P9-EGL-892

Also by Geraldine A. Ferraro

FERRARO: MY STORY

CHANGING HISTORY: WOMEN, POWER, AND POLITICS

FRAMING A LIFE

• A FAMILY MEMOIR •

Geraldine A. Ferraro

WITH

CATHERINE WHITNEY

A LISA DREW BOOK

SCRIBNER

A LISA DREW BOOK/SCRIBNER
1230 Avenue of the Americas
New York, NY 10020

Designed by Colin Joh
Set in Galliard

Manufactured in the United States of America

1 3 5 7 9 10 8 6 4 2

Library of Congress Cataloging-in-Publication Data

Ferraro, Geraldine.
Framing a life: a family memoir/Geraldine Ferraro; with Catherine Whitney.
p. cm.
"A Lisa Drew book."
Includes index.
1. Ferraro, Geraldine. 2. Women legislators—United States—Biography. 3. Legislators—United States—Biography. 4. Ferraro, Geraldine—Family. 5. Ferraro family. 6. Italian American Women—Biography. 7. United States. Congress. House—Biography. I. Whitney, Catherine (Catherine A.) II. Title.
E840.8.F47F47 1998
973.927'092—dc21
[B] 98-33813
CIP

ISBN 0-684-85404-X

To the women who frame my life:

Maria Giuseppa Caputo Corrieri
my grandmother

Antonetta Corrieri Ferraro
my mother

Donna Zaccaro Ullman and Laura Zaccaro Lee
my daughters

Natalie Ullman
my granddaughter

ACKNOWLEDGMENTS

Much has been written about the immigrant experience in America. However, until I began my personal search, I never fully appreciated the tremendous courage and sacrifice of my Italian ancestors, who left behind the certainty of their homelands for a life of promise in America. Their dreams came true, not for themselves, but through me and others like me who reaped the rewards of their hard work and unflagging resolve.

Writing this book is my way of honoring my family and celebrating the immigrant heritage that all Americans share. I could not have accomplished it without the encouragement and support of many people.

I am particularly grateful to the family members and friends who shared their recollections, insights, photographs, and enthusiasm. My sister-in-law, Teresa; my cousins and my mom's cousins, from both sides of the family: Carlo Andrisani and his wife Giovanna, Gaetano Andrisani, Dante Caputo, Tony Caputo, Fred Caputo, Jane Cerella, Tommy Corrieri, Millie Greco Montellaro, Anita Guiliano, Frances and Nick Mercardante, Patrick Mercardante, Patricia Montalto Gannon, Maria Tartaglione, her husband Angelo, and their daughter Sonja. They helped me piece together the story of my family—from Caputos to Corrieris to Ferraros and beyond. And, as always, I depend upon the enthusiasm and support of my daughters, Donna and Laura, and my daughter-in-law, Anne Rasmussen Zaccaro.

I am very thankful, too, for my friend Marylouise Oates, who encouraged me to tell the story and structure the "frame."

When I began the process of trying to retrace my grandmother's arrival in this country, I was fortunate to find several people to guide me back in time and through a labyrinth of old records: Brian G. Andersson, who, though employed with the City of New York Department of City Planning by day, pursues his avocation of tracing family trees in his off time. Without his guidance and supersleuth talent, I would never have been able to locate the passenger lists of the ships that brought my grandparents—and that provided the key to unlocking all the other details of their early lives in America. I am also grateful to Lisa Leavey in Judge Roth's chambers, who helped me locate birth and death records; Kenneth R. Cobb, director of the Municipal Archives, who got me street maps and photos of Italian

Harlem in the early days; Diane H. Dayson, superintendent, Liberty Island; Paul Sigrist Jr., director of the Ellis Island Oral History Project, who provided me with transcripts of oral history from people who arrived at the same time as my grandparents or who lived in the same neighborhood as my mother when she was a child; Jay Mazur, president of UNITE, who provided details of life in the garment factories of New York at the beginning of this century; Sister Anne Gibson, O.P., at Mount Saint Mary's in Newburgh; Father Keith Fennessy, the new pastor of Old Saint Patrick's on Mott Street; Ruth Abram of the Tenement Museum; Regina M. Calcaterra, for her excellent work researching the history of the Italian American community; Mark Bowden of the *Philadelphia Inquirer,* who gave me the research he had done for another book at another time; Jerre Mangione and Ben Morreale, whose book, *La Storia,* aided my quest for a portrait of the Italian immigrant experience; and Valentine Rippa, who assisted with research in Italy.

Of course, the whole project would not have come together without Lisa Drew, vice president and publisher, Lisa Drew Books, Scribner. Lisa not only believed that this was a story worth telling, but she put me together with the perfect person who could help me tell it, Catherine Whitney. Catherine is a talented writer and probably the most flexible and accommodating person I know. She worked around my Senate campaign schedule, through my moods, and even sent her son, Paul Whitney, a photographer and writer traveling in Italy, and his friend Michelle Gross to visit my father's home in Marcianise, interview his family, and take pictures.

I also appreciate the work of my lawyer, Bob Barnett, and Catherine's literary agent, Jane Dystel, in smoothing the way for the book to be completed; as well as Paul Krafin and Lynn Lauber, for their many hours spent helping to shape this manuscript.

Framing a Life focuses on the special contribution that women have made in shaping the American dream in this century. In 1890, when my grandmother arrived in New York, she could only sign her name with an *X*. Today, her great-granddaughter—my daughter—is an M.D. who signs prescriptions. We owe a debt of gratitude to strong women like my grandmother and my mother who made our achievements possible. However, I am also tremendously grateful for the men in my family who have enriched my life in countless ways—my father, Dominick Ferraro; my husband, John Zaccaro; my son, John Zaccaro Jr.; my two sons-in-law, Paul Ullman and Josh Lee; and my grandson, Matthew Ullman.

CONTENTS

I'll love

Learn little girl before you grow old.

For learning is better than silver or gold.

Silver and gold will vanish away.

But a good education will never decay.

Love Mother

you always

To Gerry my

Lots of Good luck

Love Grandmother.

(X)

grand child

Two pages from my 1946 autograph book.

• PROLOGUE •

My Mother's Hands

On the wall of my office hangs a photograph of my mother and me that is my favorite. It was taken shortly after the 1984 Democratic convention, in San Francisco, where I had accepted the nomination of my party as Walter Mondale's vice presidential running mate. I was forty-eight at the time, my mother seventy-nine.

As much as she had wanted to be with me, my mother could not overcome her fear of flying and attend the convention. But she was waiting for me at the airport when I returned to New York, and the swarm of media cameras caught our joyful reunion on film.

In the photo, we are wrapped in a tight embrace, my mother's head resting against my shoulder, her face shining with sheer bliss. My mother was a tiny woman, not even five feet tall, and by then the ravages of osteoporosis had diminished her even more. The angle of the photograph makes me seem the stronger one in every way. Although I am only five feet, four inches tall myself, I tower over my mother, and my protective hold gives the impression that I am her caretaker. But pictures never tell the entire truth. Our relationship was so much more complex than that.

When I look at this picture, which I often do, my eyes are inevitably drawn to my mother's gnarled, arthritic hands. One clutches my shoulder. The other is pressed against my back. Those hands tell a story.

My mother, Antonetta Ferraro, was a crochet beader. From the time she was fourteen, her fingers were busy, working deftly, her body bent forward over the large wooden beading frame. She crocheted spangles and imitation pearls, glittering pieces of glass, onto the satins, silks, and chiffons worn to weddings, galas, and balls.

She had no glitter in her life, but Antonetta did have a design in her head—a design that imitated the success stories of other immigrant families. She understood the value of education, not just for my brother, Carl, but for me, the daughter, the girl. She fashioned my life, my future, in the same way she worked the fabrics—carefully, with a skillful eye.

My nomination to the second-highest office in the land was her proudest moment. When I stood in front of the delegates and spoke about my immigrant heritage, I was overcome by the feeling that this moment belonged to her and to her mother more than it belonged to me. I remember how much I wanted to reach out with every word and hand them a return on their investment.

I knew in my heart that I would not be standing on that stage had my grandmother Maria Giuseppa Caputo not stood in steerage with her maiden aunt on the SS *Italia* and crossed to America in 1890. I would not have had the resources to run for Congress in 1978 if my mother, Antonetta Ferraro, hadn't impressed upon me the value of education, a privilege she herself was denied. Like countless others from my generation, I reaped the benefits of the sacrifices and hard labor of my immigrant legacy. I was the beneficiary of my mother's dreams—the ones she could not keep for herself but saved for me as a remarkable trousseau.

It occurs to me that the pioneers are never themselves heralded as heroes. They clear the path so that others may make a safe journey to their destination. Yet it is they who take the risks, who suffer to advance their dreams. By the time I had achieved the full potential of the American dream, it was no longer unthinkable that a woman could sit in Congress, become vice president or even president. Others had fought the worst battles before me. I stood on their backs to reach the gold ring. By the time my own two daughters embarked on their careers, in business and in medicine, the paths to their goals were already well worn.

It took me most of my lifetime to understand that my grandmother and my mother were my true role models. It wasn't readily apparent. My grandmother was Italian, bound by language and tradition to a world I never knew. My mother was a first-generation Italian American, straddling the past and the future—serving as a bridge between the two worlds. She could speak to her mother in her language and to me in mine. But I was all American, a modern woman, impatient with the past. My focus was on the future. I was eager to break free of the restrictions that women like my grandmother and mother experienced. I deemed these limitations intolerable. My grandmother and mother had been raised in eras when education and independence were not considered, or even desirable, for women. Dominated by strong men, they fell naturally into supporting roles. Constrained as they were by the daily task of caring for others, their identities did not belong to them but to their husbands, their children, and to large extended families with never-ending needs.

They were also controlled by the most powerful force of all—a set of cultural customs and mandates that belonged to another world, across the ocean, but had planted itself firmly in the tight-knit immigrant communities of America. From the time I was a young girl, I carried the warning in my head, stated over and over again: Don't step outside the lines. People will talk. (It was considered the worst thing in the world for people to talk!) Women's lives were consumed by invisible but very real boundaries. That is why my grandmother, a beautiful, high-spirited girl of fifteen, did not object to marrying a man nearly old enough to be her father—a widower with a child. The maiden aunt she had accompanied to America died soon after their arrival, and my grandmother's options disappeared. Her future was arranged for her by others, and she accepted her plight. She became a child bride and stepmother and went on to bear nine children of her own.

Cultural expectations controlled my mother's fate as well. Although she was bright and she desperately loved school, she hid her disappointment when her mother made her quit at age fourteen and sent her to work in the garment district because the family needed her paycheck.

When I was young, I recognized and appreciated the sacrifices of my mother and grandmother, but I felt certain that these were not models I ever wanted to follow. From my earliest memory I knew I could do whatever I wanted to do. I lived in a world without limits. I was the first female in my family to go to college, and I attended with Irish, German, and Polish girls who were the first in theirs as well. We didn't have much money, but we were not restricted by the times or by our ethnic backgrounds.

That is why, when I was asked in interviews over the years who my role model was, I always had a ready answer—Eleanor Roosevelt. Eleanor Roosevelt symbolized everything a woman could be: strong, educated, compassionate, independent, a force to be reckoned with in a man's world. I met her once when I was newly married and living in Manhattan. She spoke at a local community center, and after her speech I eagerly approached her to tell her how much I enjoyed hearing her. She smiled at me graciously, and I was struck by how tall she was. Indeed, she seemed to be larger than life. Eleanor Roosevelt was a very *American* model for the opportunity that was unique to American women. Had anyone suggested that I look for role models in my own immigrant heritage, I wouldn't have understood. I revered my mother, I honored my grandmother—but role models?

It took a painful moment to show me the truth.

In 1989, my mother was taken to the emergency room because she was having trouble breathing. She had previously been diagnosed with emphysema. I remember standing to the side in the room as the admissions nurse asked questions and filled out a form. At one point, she asked my mother if she had graduated from high school. My mother quickly answered, "No, but I graduated from elementary school." Then she looked down at her hands and gave a self-deprecating and embarrassed little shrug. "Big deal, huh?"

I ran to hug her, to protect her from her shame. I was stunned by my mother's verdict on herself, and I was heartbroken that I had never managed to convey that she was indeed a very big deal. I assured her that she had made an important contribution to the world. She had done so much for so many people. She was the strongest woman I knew, and smarter than most Ph.D.'s. "Besides," I added, "can you name one other person, male or female, who has been to Harvard or Yale or any other university, who can say, 'My daughter was a candidate for vice president of the United States'? Only you."

She smiled at that, but I wished I had the words to say more. My mother's contribution to the world and to me was so much greater than I could articulate. I realized that every paycheck she brought home, every hour she spent hovering over her beading frame was part of a historic tapestry.

Big deal, huh? Her sad little shrug still haunts me. Maybe I shouldn't have been so surprised. Our country still looks down on immigrant women and their offspring—those who struggled in a new land so that their children could have more. We accept opportunity as our birthright and so carelessly toss aside those whose sacrifice made it possible. I know that this very day there are fresh new waves of immigrant women who are putting aside their personal dreams so that their children can thrive in this new land. But our collective heart has grown increasingly hardened. There is a renewed backlash against immigrants, an effort to devalue them.

I was forced, in that moment in the hospital, to confront my own casual attitudes about the women who had been responsible for my many opportunities. I was ashamed that I had not boldly declared to interviewers that my mother was my role model, my grandmother was my role model. How could I not have seen it?

I began at that moment my plan to write this book—to correct my mother's impression of herself as no big deal and also to correct the nation's dismissal of the contribution of immigrant women. What is the measure of a woman's life? What achievements entitle her to be called great? I believe that my mother and her mother were great women, but my belief is driven by more than family love and loyalty. These women were part of a movement that changed the course of this century for all women. I wanted to learn as much as I could about their powerful legacy.

When I told my mother I was going to write this book, she was perplexed. "Why would you want to write about my life?" she asked. "Gerry, you're the one who has the interesting stories to tell." But I was drawn by a different kind of fascination from that which attracts one to famous people, or big, flashy events, or tales of meeting presidents and kings. This story lives in small, mundane moments and what we can read in them. They are vivid and recognizable because they are about us and who we are.

I didn't know how hard it would be to piece together the frame of my history. I felt like an archaeologist trying to excavate without a compass. I was taking a journey I had never taken before, and I felt a new humility. I had no idea where to begin, where to look. Like others in my generation, I had simply taken for granted the stories of the immigrants arriving in America—the ships with their crowded steerages, the first thrilling glimpse of the Statue of Liberty, the passage through Castle Garden and Ellis Island. But like so many others, I knew few of the actual details. Our relatives were so intent on becoming American they said little of what came before. Even my father, Dominick Ferraro, an immigrant himself, spoke sparingly about his transition to America, and he died when I was eight, taking his recollections with him. Although much has been written about the immigrant experience in America, I saw that in only two generations, I had already stopped personalizing it. My children would have no connection unless I retrieved it. It became my passion. I haunted the concrete remnants of the past, searching for names on ship rolls, marriage and birth records, death records, Census Bureau reports. I visited 250 Mott Street, where my grandmother and her aunt first lived when they arrived in New York. I interviewed my mother in the years before her death, extracting with great difficulty her earliest memories. Slowly I put the pieces together and tried to breathe life into the cold documents.

I felt all along that I was doing more than putting together a personal family history. I have spent most of my adulthood in public life, and I instinctively connect the personal with the political. The story of my grandmother and my mother is a tale of the culture that belongs to them and to me, the three of us—Italian, Italian American, American. But it is more than just our story. These women were transformed by the America they met, but they also changed the country they adopted.

When I talk to groups of women about my mother and my grandmother, their faces take on a misty quality; there is a sense of recognition at the gut level. In most families, if you go back one or two generations, you will find the same stories—the small triumphs and tragedies of immigrants grinding out lives in coal towns, crowded sweatshops, frostbitten farms.

Now, on the brink of entering a new century, we come to a unique time in America. From our standpoint of prosperity, we can look back and examine the gifts of mothers and fathers and grandparents who performed heroic deeds and suffered unthinkable sacrifices so that we could stand tall at this moment. It is an existential search, the result of our longing for identity—and our longing, too, to carry some of their greatness into our future.

So here, in these pages, I struggle to articulate what Maria Giuseppa Corrieri, Antonetta Ferraro, and their families can tell us about our future as we look into their pasts. I offer them as role models for generations of American women whose lives of opportunity were held in their work-worn hands.

As the granddaughter of a woman who never learned to write her own name, the daughter of a mother who left school for a beading frame in New York's garment district, I do not forget that their sacrifices have brought me where I am today. How can any of us forget?

• ONE •

THE JOURNEY

When my grandmother immigrated to the United States in 1890, she left behind in Italy a nearly medieval life, traditional and family centered. In the village of Terranova in southern Italy, her family lived in a one-room house on a narrow cobblestone street where she helped her mother bake bread, make pasta, and care for her younger siblings. Life was lived primarily out of doors, and farming was the chief occupation. Terranova was surrounded by a wall originally built as protection from marauding pirates; Maria's father, Ferdinando Caputo, left its boundaries each morning to tend grapevines on his plot of mountain land. It was a tough life, little changed in centuries. Feudalism lingered, the church was powerful, and life spans were short. After a visit to Sicily, Booker T. Washington declared that he found the conditions of southern Italian peasants more dire than those of Negro farmers in the southern United States.

My grandmother's maiden aunt, Maria Antonia Caputo, then

forty-seven, prevailed upon her brother and sister-in-law to allow Maria Giuseppa, fifteen, to accompany her to the New World, believing, like most Europeans, that America was a land of unlimited wealth, a growing nation where there was always work for willing hands. She didn't know that the lives of most Italian immigrants were hardly rags-to-riches stories. The majority of them lived in poverty and had gained the reputation for working hard in treacherous conditions for little pay. In spite of this, the numbers of immigrants from southern Italy dwarfed those of any other region until the beginning of World War I. My grandmother and her aunt were part of an exodus of women who would put their skills to work in textile mills, garment manufacturing, and domestic service, quietly transforming an American economy that took little note of them. Indeed, my grandmother's modest hope in crossing the Atlantic was not for adventure or education, but that she might find a job cleaning the homes of the rich. For this she kissed her family goodbye and embarked on her voyage, not knowing if she would ever see them again.

Crossing the Atlantic by ship was in itself an ordeal and took nearly a month. The only passage emigrants like my grandmother could afford was in steerage class. It was so named because the dank and fetid holds were located next to the din of the steering equipment and engines, below the waterline. Passengers traveled with freight and were overcrowded to a dangerous degree, with each compartment holding at least three hundred people. Food was inedible or inadequate, and there was no provision for washing dishes. Passengers often had to share their meager deck space with crew members butchering livestock for first-class passengers' meals. There was little privacy or sanitation, and women were routinely harassed by male passengers. Not surprisingly, many immigrants were rejected upon reaching New York—with passengers sick from cholera and other infectious diseases.

I like to think that the first face my grandmother encountered when she steamed into New York Harbor, on June 27, 1890, was that of another Italian woman. Frédéric Bartholdi had sculpted the Statue of Liberty using the face of his Italian mother as a model. Not that liberty was a concept my grandmother expected would apply to her. She brought with her the notion that a woman's life should be circumscribed by children and marriage, hard work and self-denial. As an Italian daughter, she had been raised with few personal expectations.

Her introduction to New York was a frightening one—Castle Garden, a tiny patch of land at the tip of Manhattan, the nation's first major immigrant receiving station. The fort was built before the War of 1812 to protect New York against invasion; at the time of my grandmother's arrival it had been, for several decades, a processing center. As the volume of immigrants increased, personnel at Castle Garden developed a reputation for extorting money from unsuspecting foreigners. Scam artists and thieves were also on hand to cheat naive newcomers who spoke no English and arrived vulnerable and terrified. The Castle Garden Hospital on Wards Island was eventually founded to contain the corpses of immigrants who had been detained because of ill health; they ended up being used for dissection.

Awaiting their entry papers, my grandmother and her aunt were herded into lines by junior staff, many former greenhorns themselves. New immigrants were required to have the name of a sponsor and $25 in cash to insure that they would not become dependents of the state. Since neither my grandmother nor her aunt could read or speak English, an Italian attendant read aloud the papers that were thrust in front of them, and my grandmother signed her *X*.

This country girl, illiterate and superstitious, had crossed an ocean to find herself at the edge of one of the world's greatest cities. Given the primacy of family in Italy, it is remarkable that my grandmother left so much behind for the challenges of a new life that she must have known would be onerous. Even though she was unlikely to benefit herself from the educational and vocational opportunities in America, she was a traditional Italian daughter who knew her destiny was to be a mother and wife. Perhaps it was for her future offspring and their descendants, those of us yet unborn or not even dreamed of, that she found the strength to make this difficult crossing. It's impossible to know for sure. My grandmother never spoke of it. It bears noting, however, that she and her aunt made the journey at a time when the waves of immigrants were primarily male. Of the 15 million Italian immigrants who arrived in the United States between 1875 and 1915, only about 10 percent were women. And most of these were arriving with husbands, sons, and brothers to ease the way.

My grandmother and her aunt settled into an apartment at 250 Mott Street and began their abrupt assimilation into tenement life. They could not have transported themselves to a more alien environment. The insular safety of Terranova was replaced by the anonymous, crowded world of New York. The apartment on Mott Street was certainly far worse than anything my grandmother had known in Italy. While poor in her village, she had at least had space, fresh air, sunshine, and the company of neighbors. Now she was isolated by her lack of English and confined with her aunt in a congested room. One-third of tenement rooms at that time were windowless, pitch black and without ventilation, impossible to heat in the winter or cool in the summer. Fires were common from kitchen kerosene lamps that burned for hours. Rats were so prevalent in some tenements that food had to be hung from the ceiling, and indoor plumbing was rare. Kitchens often doubled as bedrooms; bedrooms served as dining or sitting rooms.

Crammed in unsanitary conditions without bathing facilities, people were highly vulnerable to bacteria and infections. Disease flourished. Tuberculosis, the largest killer of immigrants, was a highly contagious disease that particularly flourished in airless rooms. Immigrants, moreover, brought with them Old World notions that contributed to the outbreak of disease—injunctions against winter baths and opening windows to night air, even in the hottest weather.

Only nine months after their arrival, my grandmother's aunt took to her bed with high fevers and chills—malaria. Immigrants were struck particularly hard by American epidemics; they were not only suspicious of health care provided by American charities but often too prideful to use it. In eight days Maria Antonia was dead.

Burial by the state was considered by immigrants to be the worst possible fate, but it was the destiny of Maria Antonia, who was buried in an unmarked grave designated for the poor in Calvary Cemetery, Queens. My teenage grandmother buried her alone, without the support or sympathy she would have had at home, and worried that she would never be able to locate the grave again. Having lost her one anchor in this foreign world, she was terrified. Returning home to Italy wasn't an option. She didn't have the money to make the treacherous journey back across the sea. She was stranded in America.

At sixteen, my grandmother had blossomed into a trim beauty, with a Gibson girl bun on top of her head. But as an unskilled immigrant without connections, her prospects were bleak. The older women of the neighborhood clustered around to advise her. It was impossible for her to live alone, but none of them had room to accommodate her in their already crowded apartments. Only one solution appeared feasible—and he happened to live a block away, on 250 Elizabeth Street. Domenico Corrieri , a slight, fair-haired widower sixteen years her senior, was looking for a wife. At thirty-two, my grandfather was himself an immigrant, who had lived in New York since his arrival, on the SS *Rhynland,* on Christmas Eve 1881. Left with a three-year-old daughter, Savaria, when his wife died in childbirth, he was in dire need of a wife, a mother for his child.

This match, intended as a marriage of convenience, was much

more than that for my grandfather, who was captivated by Maria at first sight. For her part, she offered no resistance to Domenico's courtship. Most immigrant women married out of a desire for financial security. For the majority it was an escape from poverty or an unpleasant family life. Marriage was not expected to include companionship, romance, or even common experience.

On May 5, 1891, only six weeks after the death of her aunt, my grandmother married my grandfather in a civil ceremony at City Hall; three weeks later they were married before God at Old Saint Patrick's Cathedral, on Mulberry Street. My grandmother's walk down the aisle under vaulted ceilings may have been her most glorious moment. Later that year, on October 23, Domenico and (by extension) his wife were sworn in as citizens of the United States. My grandmother must have felt that marriage had saved her life.

In the next year, my grandmother moved with Domenico and his young daughter to another apartment, on Mott Street. There was a practical reason for the move. At the time, with burgeoning real estate and an abundance of empty apartments, landlords were vying for tenants. As an incentive, one month's free rent was given for a one-year lease.

In this second apartment, the Corrieris started their own family, beginning with Giovannina in 1894, who was followed by Gennaro and Carmela. By the time Vincenza arrived, in 1900, the family was ready to leave the old neighborhood behind, trading the crowded streets of Little Italy for the newer tenements of uptown Manhattan, in an area known as Italian Harlem. They rented a small three-room apartment on East Ninety-seventh Street at a time when there was open farmland across the street. Without realizing it, the family was following an Italian immigrant path so clear that it could have been drawn on a map. They began downtown in Little Italy before moving up the island of Manhattan to neighborhoods in Harlem, or to Bensonhurst, in Brooklyn, or to Astoria, in Queens—to the end of the line wherever the subway traveled. Enclaves of immigrants from the same region in Italy often clustered on a particular street, banding together for comfort and security and remaining there for generations. Ninety-seventh was such a street, part of a friendly neighborhood where the Corrieris were eventually surrounded by relatives. Neighbors sang in backyards; doors were always open. Streets were crowded with horse-drawn wagons delivering ice and coal and pushcarts selling fruits and vegetables. In the back alleys, organ grinders were thrown pennies from open windows. In the evenings, lamplighters arrived with their torches to illuminate the night.

In 1907, my grandmother was joined by her sister Frances and her brother Angelo, who began his life in America selling ice from a pushcart, a business that would eventually send his children to college. Angelo had been lured to this country by the success stories he had heard in Italy, but he found my grandmother's life hardly a testament to them. She had borne a baby nearly every other year, and the family was struggling to survive. Large families were the norm among immigrants, with yearly pregnancies not only common but often considered a woman's expected contribution. Italian women had the highest birthrates of immigrant groups in New York in the early 1900s. But city life was unlike the rural, family-centered world they'd left behind. The harsh truth was that a large family was not an asset in an urban area like New York.

By 1911 my grandmother had borne Domenico five daughters and four sons to join his daughter, Savaria, who by now had shortened her name to Sarah. My mother, Antonetta, was born in 1905, when Maria Giuseppa was thirty. The children chose nicknames that wouldn't sound too foreign. My mother, named in honor of the aunt who had brought her mother to America, became Anita or Ann. But even though the children Americanized their names and spoke English in school, at the end of the day they returned to an Italian world. In the cramped quarters of Ninety-seventh Street, the Neapolitan dialect was the only language.

Determined never to lose her children to the disease that had killed her aunt, my grandmother became well known in the neighborhood as a meticulous housekeeper, her rooms redolent with disinfectant. My most enduring sense memory of my grandmother's apartment was the heavy scent of a disinfectant called CN. Cleanliness was serious business to Maria Giuseppa. After all, she had come halfway around the world on the strength of her housekeeping talents; now she benefited her family with her own fine skills. In the tiny apartment, airless and densely packed with children, she washed clothes by hand in a large utility tub in the kitchen that also doubled for hair washings and sponge baths. Her cheese ravioli and homemade pasta were spread out over the front room bed on clean, crisp, ironed sheets. She sewed all of her daughters' clothes, including the fanciest dresses. Converting her cramped rooms into an immaculate home—without electricity or any modern conveniences—required my grandmother to make considerable use of her skills.

It is hard to imagine now how even a woman with my grandmother's drive and domestic ability could have made a comfortable home for twelve people in a three-room railroad flat. But somehow she did. I never heard my mother or any of her siblings speak of hardship. The way they lived was the way everyone else lived in that uptown enclave. They made do. The door of the apartment opened onto the kitchen, with a bedroom on each side. The bathroom, located in the hallway, was shared with another family. In the bedrooms, hooks lined the walls with the family's wardrobe hanging from them; there were no closets. Beneath the clothes, barrels of peppers soaked in vinegar—which no doubt added a certain aroma to the clothing. A coal stove in the kitchen supplied the only heat and hot water, and twice a week my grandmother would boil clothes on the stove and hang them out to dry on a line that stretched across an airway to the building next door.

The bedroom featured my grandparents' bed, along with the current infants. The remainder of the children slept on foldaway cots—

the girls in the living room and the boys in the kitchen. Every morning my grandmother would fold up the cots and stand them against the wall. Then she would make her bed, smoothing out the white spread to perfection with a broom, and placing a white sheet over the top. It is there that she laid out the rolls of handmade macaroni and ravioli. With fragrant sauces bubbling on the stove and sausages and tomatoes set out to dry on the fire escape, Maria Giuseppa would set to work scrubbing the hall bathroom until it shined.

Once a week my grandfather provided each older child with a nickel to go to the bathhouse at 111th Street and Second Avenue. It was an extravagance, but he had a good year-round job as a street cleaner that was the envy of his compatriots, a prestigious position that placed him on the city payroll and provided a steady income. He managed to earn enough so that his children could receive eighth grade diplomas, a sizable accomplishment at the time, signifying competence in reading and simple arithmetic, and a knowledge of geography and history.

Of all the benefits America offered its first-generation immigrants, this was one of the most valued, though even an eighth grade education was beyond the expectations of many girls.

My mother adored her father, but he was unpopular with his wife's relatives, especially the ones who had moved into other apartments along Ninety-seventh Street. He was so jealous of his pretty younger wife that he complained even when women friends stopped by the apartment, and he forbade my grandmother to go out alone, even to church. Such was his distaste for my grandmother's relatives that it was said he cursed at them if they passed him on the street. Perhaps his intense jealousy was a natural result of my grandmother's stunning beauty and charm. An older man not much taller than his wife, Domenico might have felt that her loyalty was at risk, although the idea is preposterous. My grandmother, who was known otherwise as a proud woman and a strict disciplinarian, deferred to her husband and tried to please him, demonstrating the combination of steel and obsequiousness common to women of her generation. She was in charge of home and children; otherwise, his word was law.

Elsewhere, my grandfather was not so powerful. One day while he was at work sweeping the streets, a woman opened a window and threw a bag of garbage in the street. When it splattered on the sidewalk in front of him, he looked up and yelled at her in Italian. She called down, "Wop, I'll have you fired." And she did.

Italian immigrants, especially from the south, were considered inherently lower class by other Americans, and they were a common target of abuse. In New York, where the Irish were more established and controlled the Catholic Church and the political machinery, discrimination against Italian Americans was codified—expressed both formally and informally.

The ugly slur "wop," an acronym for "without papers," was indicative of the anti-Italian sentiment of the period. It portrayed the immigrants as illiterate, uncivilized people, foreign looking and smelling of garlic, who flooded the American shores—penniless and lacking proper documents. The prejudice was so deep rooted that it exists to this day, passed along from generation to generation.

My grandfather's job loss was devastating for him. The dominant status of the immigrant father was maintained by his role as provider and protector of his family. Despite anti-immigrant discrimination practices and economic conditions, he rarely failed in this role. Family survival was considered more important than pride or personal gratification. After my grandfather was fired, he still got up every morning to search for work, at such projects as the Sixth Avenue Elevated and the Queens Midtown Tunnel. Manual labor, however, required a youthful vigor that he no longer possessed. Several years later, he was disabled by a stroke and unable to work again. My grandmother claimed that this illness was a direct result of the hard labor he was forced to perform after he was fired.

Although he identified himself in 1920 as a steamship laborer, this was the statement of a still-proud man unable to tell the census taker the truth. He spent his later years barely able to speak, a sad presence in the middle of a busy household where he had once been the breadwinner.

• TWO •

Hard Labor and Foolish Dreams

Although my grandmother could not have realized it at the time, one of her most momentous acts was pulling my mother out of school after the eighth grade and sending her to work. This was an event that not only shaped my mother's life but had far-reaching implications for my own. My mother loved school. She was very intelligent, and she had big dreams.

"When I grow up, I'm going to have a car and a house and a maid, and my children are going to have fine clothes," she told her mother.

"Ah, Antonetta," she laughed. "Such silly dreams."

My mother wasn't dissuaded. She was a cheerful, bright, curious little girl, a good student who was confident of her path.

I don't know if the abrupt end to my mother's education came as a surprise to her, or if she knew all along that as a girl she couldn't expect to go on to high school—only the rare few in her circle did that. However, as she approached her eighth grade graduation, her mother broke the news. Her education was over. The family needed her to go to work.

When she heard that my mother was quitting school, the principal of P.S. 150 visited the family and advised that my mother continue her education. My grandmother refused. With my grandfather ill, they were counting on Antonetta's income. Since family welfare was considered the primary responsibility of each of its members, children were expected to contribute to its support as soon as they were able. She also refused the principal's suggestion that perhaps Antonetta might attend school at night. By my grandmother's standards, it was highly improper for a young woman to be out in the evening. The principal had yet a third suggestion—secretarial school. It would be a shorter course and would result in a better job. But my mother's brother-in-law Tom, who was married to her sister Millie, dealt the fatal blow to that idea. "You know what secretaries do," he scoffed. "They sit on the boss's lap." His casual words sealed my mother's fate.

I often think that if my mother had continued her schooling and been nurtured, as I was, by women of intellect and ideals, her future might have been different. There is evidence that she and her young friends at P.S. 150 were already shaking off their immigrant roots, eager to take on roles as American women without limits. After my mother died, I came across her eighth grade autograph book, filled with words of love and hope penned in the neat girlish script of her fourteen-year-old friends. Between the covers, crumbling with age, were the visions of those still young enough to have dreams. It was the style of the day to construct a little rhyme. The entries were sweet and sentimental, and most of them wished my mother nothing more than a successful marriage, but several implied a sharp prefeminist bent. I laughed when I read one of them:

When you are married
And your husband is cross
Pick up the broom
And say I'm the boss.
Your friend,
Rose Ciafone

Another read—poignantly, I thought, since most of the girls were leaving school that year—

Learn little girl before you grow old
For learning is better than silver or gold.
Silver or gold may vanish away
But a good education will never decay.
Your loving friend and sister grad-u-8
Rose Soloway

On the back cover of the autograph book, my mother had carefully listed the names of all thirty-nine students in Miss Ruth I. Patterson's graduating class. Almost all the names are recognizably Jewish—Brodsky, Edelstein, Berger, Levinsohn, Heller, Schwartz, Weiss. Jewish parents placed a premium on education that was not echoed in Italian families. The class roster contains only three Italian names, including that of Antonetta. I have to assume, in a neighborhood crowded with Italian kids and a school with only a sprinkling of Italian names, that most of them didn't even make it to the eighth grade.

It was no surprise that my grandmother saw education as exotic and impractical. She had survived in America since she was a teenager without even learning the alphabet. Cocooned in the close-knit enclave of Italian Harlem, she saw no need to learn English. Notions of youthful freedom and women's rights were dismissed by immigrants as *americanate,* and any efforts on the part of teachers to Americanize children were resented as intrusions on the family. My mother adapted to her fate, however reluctantly, never speaking of whatever ambitions she might have harbored.

My grandmother, so fearful of the outside world, was sending her fourteen-year-old daughter into a far more dangerous arena than secretarial school. The garment district was a tough place to work, with long hours, few breaks, and unsafe conditions. It had been only eight years since the infamous fire at the Triangle Shirtwaist Company off Washington Square, where 146 employees, most of them young women, lost their lives. Safety violations in the crammed, filthy factories were legend; girls were jammed into noisy, unventilated rooms to labor on dangerous machinery. Fire escapes were broken or nonexistent, and the women were frequently locked in during working hours.

Many Italians labored in the sweatshops of lower Manhattan. A large proportion of these workers were women, who were paid lower wages than men. For female immigrants, there was always this double inferiority—at home as a woman, in America as an immigrant.

My mother entered the workplace with a specialty, crochet beading, learned from a neighbor who did piecework in a nearby apartment. Beaded items had grown popular with the advent of the flapper, and my mother's skill was much in demand. Each morning my mother took the Third Avenue El to the garment district with her sister Jencie, who worked nearby making children's caps. She spent the day angled over a crochet frame, a position that left her bent in old age. After work, she and Jencie returned home together. The first thing my mother did at the end of every month was hand my grandmother her unopened pay envelope. Girls were typically expected to contribute more than their brothers to the household expenses, turning over their entire pay. In this and other ways, there was disparity between boys and girls in immigrant families, where the notion of male superiority was carried over from Europe.

Whatever my mother's dreams had been during her carefree years as a schoolgirl, she now rerouted her hopes to the glamorous world of the silent movie matinees she attended on Saturdays—where women went to work for independence and married for love.

But earning a living did not make her independent. Even though it was the beginning of the Roaring Twenties, her activities outside of work were regulated by my grandmother. Just as my grandfather had forbidden my grandmother to go anywhere alone, now my grandmother restricted my mother's movements, permitting her to leave the house only in the company of her sisters. Since a successful marriage match was more dependent on a spotless reputation than on a large dowry, girls were supervised at all times as a matter of course. Italians were notorious for their conservative views in sexual matters. Kissing was considered by some an American custom: not allowed before marriage and, some claimed, rarely engaged in afterward. My mother's parents were said to be reserved around one another, to the point of seeming embarrassed. There was no hint of a romantic spark, or any of the flirtatious teasing my husband and I have engaged in, even in front of our children.

There were rigid rules separating the sexes. My mother was not allowed to go to dance halls or swim at the municipal pool three blocks from their apartment. But she was strong willed. In spite of these limitations, her spirit still managed to shine. She bobbed her hair and waded at Coney Island; she mastered the Charleston, learning the steps by watching vaudeville acts at Saturday matinees. Forbidden to visit dance halls, she danced at family parties, festivals, and feast days instead, adapting to her circumstances as her mother had done.

Although most of her income went for support of the family, some was put aside for the only event that could transport her out of a life of unskilled labor and into the world of affluence and comfort she dreamed of. That event was marriage. A young woman's world revolved around her eventual courtship, with hope chests begun in early childhood. No decision she ever made would be as important as her choice of whom she married; it was possibly the only significant decision she would make in her life. Even with the difference in their generations, this reality remained much the same for my mother and grandmother. Just as my grandmother looked to marriage to save her as a newcomer in a foreign country, so my mother saw it as her eventual path to a wider world. The difference was that my mother decided against an arranged marriage. She would marry for love or not at all.

In spite of living in the middle of an impersonal city, most immigrant families managed to preserve certain aspects of the provincial world they had left behind. San Gennaro, the patron saint of Naples, the area where my grandparents were from, was honored every September. But it was the feast of Our Lady of Mount Carmel that was most significant for women like my mother and grandmother. This celebration was of such importance and attracted so many worshipers that Pope Leo XIII elevated Mount Carmel Church on 115th Street to the status of a shrine. This festival united young and old women before the Madonna, a figure who not only sanctified their lives but could heal and understand them. This was a powerful, personal Madonna, both the Mother of God and an example of a purity that parents were anxious to preserve in their young women. The feast was a rare public proclamation of the power and authority of women and also a reminder that their appropriate sphere was in the home.

On July 15, the eve of the feast of Our Lady of Mount Carmel, the women of the family met at my grandmother's apartment. From there they joined a sea of other women who streamed barefoot out of their homes and took over the streets of Italian Harlem. A float carrying a large statue of the Madonna and surrounded by schoolgirls and young women dressed in white was pulled through the streets by devotees. Penitents were at the rear of the procession, some crawling on hands and knees until they reached the church on 115th Street, which opened its doors at midnight. All night, waves of women took their places at the altar. Some sat vigils that lasted throughout the night; others moved on hands and knees down the aisle of the church. In this way women were called both to affirm and atone for their own power.

By 1927, all the Corrieri daughters had married except my mother. Petite, charming, and pretty, she was also twenty-two years old, approaching a dangerous age, according to my grandmother, who complained that she was "too picky" in turning down the young men she met at family parties. But Antonetta had decided that she was going to hold on to her ideals as far as a husband was concerned. Even though the circle of suitors acceptable to her family was strictly limited by her culture, she would not marry until she was in love. This resolve cost my mother her dowry. Always generous to a fault, she took the money she had saved and used it to purchase a trousseau for her sister Anna, who was two years younger and ready to marry.

Dominick Ferraro—affluent, darkly handsome, from a family of educated landowners and professionals—made his remarkable appearance into this closed pond of suitors as if in answer to my mother's yearnings. He had immigrated in 1920 on a growing swell of anti-immigration sentiment. The rise of Mussolini and his Fascists gave exclusionist forces the chance to brand all Italians as radicals. In fact, upon his arrival Dominick was asked whether or not he was an anarchist. By coincidence, he came from Marcianise, a village near the Salerno region (where my grandmother Maria Giuseppa's mother and father were born). The Ferraro family was wealthy and prominent. My paternal grandfather was an engineer, known to the peasants who worked his property as Don Carlo—Don, a term of respect given to landowners and men of prominence. My grandmother, Maria Alessandra, was half French. Her father had been the landscape architect who, I am told, designed the gardens at the king's summer palace at Caserta. My mother told me that my grandfather had seen Maria Alessandra Lener at a party and had fallen in love with her because of her striking blue eyes.

Dominick's family had plans for his future, but he was drawn to America and left Italy after a year at university to seek his fortune. He was part of an exodus of young bachelors, often the younger sons of large families, who departed Italy as soon as they were of legal age, thus freeing themselves of their father's dominance while embarking on a path to personal liberty.

In Italy my father would never have been able to marry my mother, such were the economic and social differences between the two families. He arrived not as a poor immigrant but with the money, experience, and connections to eventually set himself up in the restaurant business. By the time he met my mother, in May 1927, he was already a prosperous citizen, the embodiment of all my mother had hoped for in a husband. Here was the man—handsome, mannerly, and devoted—who finally deserved her.

Even my grandmother was charmed by Dominick's polite attentiveness, though not enough to drop her vigilance entirely. She still insisted that a niece or nephew chaperone the couple to dinner and Broadway shows. This did not dissuade Dominick. He appeared at dinner one evening so certain of my mother's affections that he presented her with an engagement ring without even bothering to propose. Antonetta cried, "Oh, my God, what's this?"

"An engagement ring," Dominick replied with a grin.

At this, my grandmother finally let down her great guard. She kissed Dominick and announced they would celebrate. After summoning her other daughters to the apartment on Ninety-seventh, she fried pizza dough and prepared homemade *zeppole,* which were consumed with gusto.

Although she was engaged, until the day of her marriage there were still restrictions placed on my mother. One of these probably saved her life. Because she was forbidden to accompany my father to a party in the country one Sunday in June, Dominick went with Anna's husband, Charles Maddi, instead. It was on this trip that my father had the first of the auto accidents that would haunt my parents' lives. At a curving intersection on Route 9W between Milton and Newburgh, New York, my father failed to negotiate a sharp turn and crashed into a stone wall. In danger of bleeding to death, he was rushed to Saint Luke's Hospital, where his wounds required forty-eight stitches to close. Charles was also injured, though less badly. When it was time for the bandages to be removed from Dominick's face, he brought his doctor to my grandmother's apartment on Ninety-seventh Street.

The doctor said to my mother and grandmother, "Be prepared. He's going to have scars."

The doctor began removing the bandages. As soon as the first one came off, my father saw the scars over his eye and temple, and cried to my mother: "Go out of the room. Leave me! I don't want you to see it!"

Dominick no longer looked like the man Antonetta had agreed to marry. There was no chance of plastic surgery; the scars that marked my father might remain for the rest of his life. Embarrassed and angry, Dominick told my mother that he would release her from their engagement. In fact, other relatives began to whisper that the accident was reason enough to call off the marriage. But my mother stood by my father with such steadfastness that it made him cry.

"When I make up my mind, nobody can change it. We are getting married," she said.

In his gratitude Dominick bought her trousseau and presented her with a dowry—both gifts kept secret from his own family, so that Antonetta would not lose face. They were married on October 2, 1927, at Saint Lucy's Church on 104th Street. Though the church on Ninety-sixth Street was closer, it was reserved for the Irish and for wealthier parishioners who lived downtown from its entrance. Italians got married in Italian Harlem. In her wedding photograph, my mother looks particularly tiny—overwhelmed by her flowing bouquet of roses and the towering man beside her, whose scars had been airbrushed from the photo.

A new home, in Astoria, awaited my mother, a corner house on Thirty-second Street, a short ferry ride across the river from her mother and relatives. Dominick had purchased the house the month before their wedding and had already placed the deed in my mother's name.

By 1928 my mother was pregnant with twin boys, who were born in March 1929, at a private hospital in Astoria, after a long and difficult labor. One of the twins experienced severe problems. Convulsions began on his second day, and the hospital routinely baptized him as Baby Boy Ferraro. Antonetta insisted that a priest be brought to the hospital and the baby be named Anthony, after Saint Anthony of Padua, a great performer of miracles. But there was no miracle for this child. On his third day, Anthony died and was buried in Calvary Cemetery in Queens, the same setting where my grandmother's aunt Maria Antonia had been laid to rest in her unmarked pauper's grave years before.

When Antonetta was fully recovered, she and Dominick traveled to Italy to show off Carl, the surviving twin, to the Ferraro family. What was planned as a short visit had to be extended to nine months when Carl came down with pneumonia. My mother was uncomfortable surrounded by servants in the wealthy Ferraro household. She was ashamed of her crude Neapolitan dialect, which sounded so unlike their educated tongue. She had never been so far from her family, and her homesickness was compounded by her concern over Carl's health. Intimidated, lonely, and now pregnant again, she suffered a miscarriage during these months. But on this trip she developed a close bond with Dominick's older brother Joseph, affectionately called Peppino. An agronomist and a city official, he tried to help Antonetta feel comfortable in the family. Each night after she put Carl to sleep, Joseph gave her Italian lessons. For the first time since the eighth grade my mother was not only permitted but encouraged to learn, and it gave her great pleasure.

Back in Astoria, my mother bore another child in 1931, a son named Gerard. This happy birth was followed two months later by the death of her father, at age seventy-three, from a cerebral hemorrhage after more than a decade of invalidism. His wake was held in the tiny apartment; for three days and three nights there was a steady stream of relatives and friends arriving to pay their respects.

Although Maria Giuseppa went into mourning and wore black for a year, Domenico's death was in many ways her emancipation. She could now escape the apartment where she had been largely confined since her marriage, in the last years also serving as her husband's nurse. Now she could at least go to Mass and board a ferry to visit Antonetta, who would soon be heading for Newburgh, after prospering in Queens.

• THREE •

The American Dream

When my parents moved with my two brothers to Newburgh, New York, in 1933, they had no way of knowing that their life would be anything but the tranquil embodiment of the American dream. Newburgh was a bustling small town on the west bank of the Hudson River, sixty miles north of the city, near enough for my mother to easily visit her family. With its fresh air, river vistas, and booming economy, it was the perfect setting for a young family with high hopes.

But even as they packed to leave Astoria, sad news arrived from Dominick's parents in Italy. His brother Joseph, the beloved Peppino who had befriended Antonetta, had been killed in an auto accident on the way back from Rome. Occurring in the shadow of my father's own accident, this was chilling news. Still, they were optimistic as they finalized their move to Newburgh. Prohibition had ended, and there was a new permissive attitude in America that my father was eager to capitalize on. Naturally gregarious and a fine cook, his dream of opening a restaurant was finally going to materialize. After satisfying the strict regulations governing liquor licensing, he found the perfect site—the ground floor of two three-story buildings he bought at the corner of Mill Street and West Parameter. He called his restaurant and bar the Roxy and moved my mother and their two young sons into the second-floor apartment, which was soon filled with long-term visitors.

From the time my mother moved to the "country," in Astoria, she had relieved her city sisters by taking nieces and nephews to stay with her for weeks at a time. She continued this practice in Newburgh, where it was expected of her as the successful sister, the one with an adoring husband, two beautiful children, and a family business. In fact the lodgings on Mill Street were luxurious compared to the apartment on Ninety-seventh Street. They were sunny and spacious with a fireplace, and there were also rental units that my parents used to help pay off their mortgage. In this small-town enclave my mother was happy to share her good fortune.

Then, in 1934, tragedy struck with yet another car accident. This was the event that was to shape so many aspects of my family's life in the years to come. And as you will see, it was a particularly pivotal event for me—although I was not yet born. It was October 13, exactly two years since the death of my mother's father. My parents and their two boys drove to Manhattan to visit Maria Giuseppa. On the way back home, Carl and a younger cousin roughhoused in the back while Gerard, three, grew cranky. He'd recently had a cold and my mother was worried about him. When she brought him into the front seat with her, he fell asleep in her arms.

It was a treacherous, rainy night on Route 9W. Near the spot where my father had crashed seven years earlier, an oncoming car suddenly lost control, veered out of its lane, and hurtled head-on into my family's car. When young Carl managed to crawl out of the wreckage, he found his mother sprawled on the ground, asleep, he thought. There was blood everywhere, and a disattached eye sat in the mud, staring sightlessly into the darkness. It belonged to Gerard. He had been killed instantly, while the others were spared. But his funeral was delayed until it was clear whether my mother would actually survive. Her spine had been severely injured, and she drifted in and out of consciousness, not learning of her son's death until several days later.

While my mother was still bedridden, Maria Giuseppa arrived from New York and insisted that Antonetta view her dead child so that she would begin accepting his death. But even after she kissed Gerard good-bye, my mother couldn't rid herself of guilt. Some family members believed that by cushioning the blows, Gerard had saved Antonetta's life with his body and cost him his own. She endlessly berated herself for bringing him into the front seat with her.

My father was unable to comfort her. He was overcome with guilt over what might have been—had he gotten out of the path of the other car in time, had he left New York earlier, had they decided to spend the night in Manhattan when the weather turned bad. As he sank into his private grief, my mother grew more depressed, week after week washing and ironing Gerard's clothes, which still hung in the closet. She haunted the cemetery, decorating the sad little grave, which now housed two boys, with Christmas trees and small toys. The doctor, noting my parents' distress, had only one recommendation—that they quickly have another child, to replace the grief of death with the joy of birth. They complied—perhaps more out of trust than desire. Still in great pain from her back injury, my mother managed to conceive again within two months of the accident.

My mother later told me that the day she conceived she was bursting with happiness, as if a light had broken through her despair. Her mother came to visit soon after and, hoping to comfort my mother over the loss of Gerard, said, "I hope it's a boy."

"Boy or girl, I don't care," my mother said with feeling. "I just want the baby to have a long life and be intelligent and beautiful."

And thus I arrived, a salve to my parents' pain, on the heels of my brother's death and six years into the Great Depression. I was born at home on August 26, 1935, because my mother would not leave Carl, her last surviving child, home alone while she went to the hospital. She was also afraid that her baby would be kidnapped or switched with another baby in the hospital. This wasn't merely superstition on her part. It was around the time of the Lindbergh kidnapping, and like other parents, she was shaken to the core by the image of the stolen baby.

I weighed in at eleven pounds, six ounces, and although I was named after my dead brother, my mother made it clear that I was not taking his place. "Gerry is special," she insisted, "because she is a girl."

If it is true that sexual equality is part of the process of becoming an American, then I am certainly that product. The restrictions placed on the women in my family through the generations stopped now, with me. I was regularly assured by my mother that I could accomplish anything. My father was so thrilled by my arrival that my mother had to stop him from throwing almost weekly birthday parties for me, afraid that I would grow up believing this was the norm. But she doted on me herself, spending hours wrapping my hair around her fingers into corkscrew curls, crocheting my dresses, and making sure my bows matched my socks. I became my father's princess and my mother's little doll, so protected that I took my first steps inside a playpen because my mother couldn't bear to see me dirtied from crawling.

My father's business was thriving, and in 1939 he moved the Roxy to a new location, next door, and converted the ground floor into a five-and-dime, where my mother went to work. It was a general store that carried everything a home might need, from pots and pans to garden tools. But my mother also took care to supply everything a woman might need to make that home a special place. In the center of the store was a large counter that held the yarn my mother used to crochet lace doilies, and multicolored threads with which to embroider dish towels and aprons. Along the wall to the left was a counter that displayed the most wonderful toys. It was all mine.

Life took on a sense of normalcy and contentment—a taste of the good life in America that was still a distant dream for so many immigrants. But only months after my father moved the Roxy, he encountered his first in a series of citations by the state liquor authorities. They claimed the Roxy was a gathering place where women, employed as entertainers in the floor show, asked men to buy them drinks. The charges were eventually dismissed.

Although I was never allowed to go into the Roxy, I spent my afternoons at the five-and-dime with my mother amid the bulk yarn and long counters of toys. It was an innocent, patriotic time. My family thought President Roosevelt spoke personally to us on the radio; for Halloween, my mother dressed me up as Miss America and Carl as Uncle Sam.

I think my parents wanted to keep me a baby for as long as they could. When I began half-day kindergarten at Mount Saint Mary's, the nuns were horrified to discover that I was still drinking my milk from a baby bottle. I was soon told in no uncertain terms that if I was such a baby, I was too young to go to school. I swore off my bottle, at least in their presence; but when my father picked me up at lunchtime, he waited until we were in the front seat of his car, away from the eyes of the good sisters, and then let me lie down and have my bottle.

Mount Saint Mary's was exactly the type of educational setting that my parents had pictured in their dreams. A good Catholic school of the highest standards, it was operated by a no-nonsense order of Dominican sisters that had originated in Regensburg, Germany. Carl attended until he was twelve and transferred to a military academy, and it was there that I received my first taste of formal learning, as well as my first encounter with strong women who did not cater to my whims.

After school my mother saw to it that I was given every possible opportunity—as if she believed she could fill the empty places in her own past with a wealth of experiences in my present. I swam, took tap dancing lessons, and played the piano throughout my childhood. When my mother sat for hours, bundled against the cold, watching me ice-skate at a nearby lake, it seemed that she was enjoying herself as much as I was.

One summer, my father, his brother Carlo, and my aunt Millie's husband, Tom, rented three bungalows for the summer at Rocky Point, on the north shore of Long Island. The women and children were there during the week, and the men would join us on the weekends. On Friday nights, the women would set up a long table on the beach and our three families would enjoy a great feast.

My cousin Anita, who stayed with us that summer, told me many years later that she still had fond memories of Rocky Point. "The first night your father came out to join us, he was so thrilled to see you children that when Carl ran to him he picked him up, swung him in the air, and kissed him," Anita recalled. "He came over to where we were sitting and he picked you up and kissed you. I looked down at the ground. My father was dead. But then I felt myself being picked up. Your father hugged me and gave me a kiss too. I felt so good. He made me feel that I was a part of the family."

My mother's best friend in Newburgh was a woman named Fannie Farina. Her daughter Helen was my age, and we were best friends, too. Our mothers would dress us exactly alike, except in different colors. If I had a light blue coat and hat, she had the same coat and hat in yellow.

Helen was adopted. Her mother told her that she and Helen's father had prayed for a baby, and one day God sent them to the New York Foundling Hospital. They looked and looked among all the babies until they spotted Helen. They knew she was perfect and they took her home.

As soon as Helen heard this story, she immediately asked, "Is Gerry adopted too?" To which Fannie replied, "No, her mother had no choice. She *had* to take her!"

Helen taunted me about that for months, feeling superior that she had been chosen while my parents were "stuck" with me.

By 1940 my father could write proudly to his own father in Italy: "I live like a king." By then he had purchased a three-story house with stained-glass windows on DuBois Street that was once the rectory for a nearby church. My mother was initially put off by the house's condition—it was filthy and smelled of mildew—but she saw the potential and set about fixing it up. In fact, it was a glorious house, with a fireplace in every room and balconies outside the windows. I had a turreted bedroom filled with fifty-three dolls, a dollhouse with real electric lights, and a vast collection of miniature dresses crocheted by my mother. The kitchen was a warm and welcoming place—the true center of life in our home. To this day I have a vivid image of my father standing over the stove, stirring his thick, fragrant gravy (our name for sauce) as Carl and I stood eagerly by waiting for a taste. When it began bubbling, he would rip off pieces of fresh Italian bread, dunk them into the pot, and hand them to Carl and me, with the gravy dripping down our hands.

My father continued to have a touching faith in America, but in many ways he remained naive about the cool impersonality of its bureaucracy. In late 1940 and early 1941, the liquor authority once again brought charges against him, repeating its claim that women who worked in the Roxy as hostesses solicited drinks from customers.

Even though the transcript of my father's hearing suggests that he had trouble understanding the exact nature of the charges against him, he was not savvy enough to have a lawyer represent him. At one point during the hearing, when he was asked if he had any objections to additional charges and amendments, he responded, sadly, "No . . . my place is nice and clean."

Left alone before a panel of state officials and investigators, he was clearly overwhelmed.

"Put me out of business means putting my family on the relief because I got nothing else to do," he told the judge. "I plead to you, Judge, give me another chance."

But the judge did not give my father another chance; two weeks later he lost his license. With no knowledge of appeals, my father's only perceived recourse was to have my mother write a personal letter to President Franklin Roosevelt, begging him to intercede on my father's behalf. Needless to say, Roosevelt never replied.

"We just didn't know how things worked," my mother said years later. "We didn't know that when we opened a bigger place, we were supposed to share our success with the police and other officials."

"But why didn't he go to the hearing with an attorney?" I asked her.

She shook her head. "Your father was too proud. In a lot of ways, he was still a foreigner. He thought that if he went to the hearing and he told the truth, he would be okay."

Although he tried to put a good face on the situation in letters home to his family, the loss of the Roxy was a blow to my father's role as chief provider for the family—not unlike the blow my grandfather suffered when he was unfairly fired from his street-sweeping job. In our case, we at least still had the five-and-dime, where my father now joined my mother each day. It is there, as he straddled a chair outside of the store, his arms draped over the back, that I have my one remaining live recollection of my father. The rest are only images from old photographs.

Despite their financial difficulties, my parents continued to send Carl to the military boarding school and to keep me in private education. Tuitions were high, but both my parents—my mother with her eighth grade education and my father with his one year of university—were insistent. If they had to work a little harder, or sacrifice, they would gladly do it for their children.

Though there were only two of us, my father was determined that we enjoy the pleasures of a large family, even if it was an extended one. Sunday was the day everyone crowded the house on DuBois Street. Church was followed by my father's special spaghetti dinner. The scent of his fragrant gravy permeated our house. We sat down to the table at three o'clock and did not get up for at least two hours. My post was always beside my father, who put a little wine in the bottom of my glass, then filled it up with cream soda.

With the advent of World War II, my father lost the possibility of visiting his family in Italy. By then he was also too old to serve in the military, but he bought savings bonds and helped my mother recycle for the war effort. Like other women during this time, my mother balanced a work life in the five-and-dime and a home life managing a victory garden, canning tomatoes and pears, and overseeing her family.

My mother watched as her two younger brothers joined the navy and as nephews went off into every branch of the service. World War II gave Italian American men fresh opportunities to prove their patriotism, especially since one arena of the war was their homeland. There was tremendous pride in our family, and in the Italian American community as a whole, in the contribution our young men made to the war effort. More than five hundred thousand Italian Americans served in the military during World War II.

But just as the war was a source of pride, so too was it a source of heartbreak. My aunt Millie's son John had joined the navy as soon as Pearl Harbor was bombed. He was shipped out to sea on the SS *Quincy,* and the ship went down. News of John's death was a tremendous shock to the family, and Aunt Millie refused to believe it. She sought the intercession of the saints for a miracle, but there was no miracle. The cold reality arrived on her doorstep with John's Gold Star. Millie died a few years after the war; everyone said the cause was a broken heart. When I visited Manila in 1989, I went to the National Cemetery and found the name Giovanni Corrieri on the Memorial Wall.

Frank Mercardante, my aunt Jennie's oldest son, was a ranger who served in the African theater. In June 1944, he was flown to England and became part of the Allies' invasion of Normandy. On the last day of the assault, when the heaviest casualties were reported, he heard the shouts of a wounded buddy from a nearby foxhole. As Frank lifted his friend onto his shoulders to carry him behind the lines, a shell exploded. Frank lost one leg, and the other was severely scarred.

Forty years after the war, I would learn that my family in Italy was making brave contributions to the war effort as well. In 1984, when I was campaigning in New Jersey during the presidential race, a man came up to me at an event. He handed me a yellowed photograph showing Uncle Angelo, my father's younger brother, standing with two GIs. "Angelo saved our lives," he said emotionally. That's how I learned that my uncle Angelo had served in the Italian Resistance.

In the last year of the war, my father settled on a business investment that he believed would be both profitable and a pleasure for me, a roller-skating rink. A few days before the deal was to be struck, he drove my brother, Carl, back to boarding school. On the way home, he stopped to play bocce with a group of his friends and then started the drive back to our house.

He never made it. A policeman found him slumped over the wheel of his car, still conscious enough to ask that my mother be called. But my mother couldn't go to him herself; one of the many skills she had been forbidden to learn was driving. Instead she called the doctor, then sent a cab to pick up her husband.

The doctor who came to the house and examined my father gave him an injection but refused to tell my mother exactly what was wrong with him. When I came into my parents' room the next morning, I found my mother holding the hand of my father, who looked at me, then turned away and died.

Even at this, her saddest moment, my mother thought of my feelings before her own. "Gerry, your father has gone to heaven," she said. "He waited for you to come in."

My father had died of a heart attack. He was forty-five years old, and I was a few months shy of nine.

• FOUR •

THE SEPARATION

There is a dividing line that runs through my life, a before and an after, and that line is marked by the death of my father. There had been a brief interlude of family happiness that gave me something to strive for in my own future. But after my father's death came the struggle, especially for my mother. She'd had some of her dream fulfilled, but it had lasted only until her thirty-ninth year.

When I was going through my mother's papers after her death, I came upon a letter she had written to my brother and me shortly after my father's fatal heart attack. She had tucked the letter away. It had never been shown to us. It was dated October 25, 1944, and when I read the words, written in her anxious scrawl, a chill ran through me.

> Dearest Gerry and Carl,
>
> Sometimes we cannot understand the way of God. Always, Gerry and Carl, live by the ten commandments of God. . . . Don't be bitter. After I am gone, children dear, don't grieve.

> Say a prayer every night, light a candle and have a Mass said once in a while, also give a little to charity in honor of your mother and dad. Don't grieve and don't mourn, for my wish is you both should be happy because at last I have gone to join your father, my husband, in an eternal life and happiness.

My first thought was to wonder if my mother had contemplated suicide in the weeks following my father's death. No, I decided, that was impossible. She would never have willingly left us. But my father's death had shaken her to the core—made her doubt whether she could survive. The letter's tone of stunned loss suggests that there was a time when she seriously questioned her ability to endure without my father by her side. My brother and I were unaware of these feelings. As always, she hid her suffering from us.

Our life of relative prosperity came to an abrupt halt with the death of my father, a fairy tale drawn to a close. I was no longer anyone's princess, and I was suddenly forced to concentrate on lessons I would never forget—the importance of always having another plan at the ready, the realization that nothing can ever be taken for granted.

Had my father lived, I would have been someone else, the girl who went from Mount Saint Mary's to finishing school, to probable marriage to a West Point cadet. My family would have remained discreetly in the background while I advanced into the better, all-American world they envisioned for me. But that was now forever changed. In my new life, there was no mistaking the dominant figure who stood beside me, steering me forward, laboring to clear my path. That figure was my mother.

Only hours after my father's death, our extended family swarmed into Newburgh, propelled on a crushing wave of grief. Carl returned home from New York Military Academy, and we were soon enveloped by a host of weeping relatives. My grandmother and several cousins stayed at our house; others drove two hours from New York City. Although my father had been carried out by the undertaker, my mother couldn't bear to leave him at the funeral home—she insisted he be laid out in our parlor, on DuBois Street, instead. My father returned home late the next day in a dark, polished coffin.

It was the end of May, and the coffin was surrounded by layered banks of flowers. They flooded the house with their overwhelming sweetness. The outpouring of sorrow was such that the wake could not be contained within set visiting hours. For three days and three nights, bereaved neighbors and friends streamed through our house to view my father's body, crying and murmuring, "So young. So young." A chair was placed beside the coffin, and my mother sat there rigidly in a black dress, receiving the hundreds of people who filed past. Carl sat slumped nearby, wearing his military uniform, tears streaming down his face. His grief was of a different nature than mine, his hurt more complex. Carl was fourteen, and his father left him just when he needed him most. I sometimes think that Carl never fully recovered.

My mother wouldn't allow me to wear black. She kept telling me that my father wouldn't have wanted me to mourn. But I didn't understand. What *would* he have wanted? How could he have gone? Why didn't he let any of us know? I stood numb and dry eyed watching my grandmother hang like a small black bird over the coffin, sobbing in Italian: "Domenico, why have you left us? What a good son you were!"

My father's death was calamitous to me, a disaster of unimaginable magnitude. How could it have happened? Had I caused it somehow? What if clambering onto his back so that he could carry me upstairs each night had precipitated his heart attack? Along with my grief I felt the sting of another painful new emotion—guilt.

My father was buried the day after Memorial Day. The Mass was held in Newburgh. Then we got into cars to drive down to Calvary

Cemetery in Queens. At Calvary, my mother held my hand as we watched the grave diggers lift the two small coffins of my brothers—Anthony, who'd died at birth, and Gerard, who'd died in my mother's arms at three—from the black earth. When my father's coffin was lowered into the ground, my brothers' small coffins were placed on top of his. The headstone eventually read: BELOVED HUSBAND AND CHILDREN.

Although it had seemed to, time didn't stop. Amazingly, the summer of 1944 arrived on DuBois Street without my father. Carl went off to Puerto Rico with his roommate to spend the summer break with his family, and my mother and I rattled around the big, empty house, inseparable yet aching with loneliness at the same time. My mother was no longer a quiet, subservient wife, modeled after her immigrant mother. Her approach to life had been transformed into an attitude that was distinctly American and ambitious. But in terms of the Catholic Church, the Old World lingered in her. At thirty-nine, she entered the role of widowhood completely. She wore black for a year, never going to a movie or turning on the radio. She believed that my father watched her grieve for him from heaven.

She knit an afghan during those first months of her bereavement. She sat in the entrance of the five-and-dime as she waited for customers and watched me play with friends. She worked her worries into the yarn, row by row, until they spilled over her lap and down her black-stockinged legs. How could she run the business, settle the accounts and mortgages, and raise my brother and me all by herself? Her solution was to ask my grandmother to move in with us.

Perhaps Newburgh was too far from Italian Harlem and the rest of the family; perhaps Maria Giuseppa had taken care of too many children with too little money for too long. Or maybe, at seventy, she didn't want to give up the first taste of independence she'd ever known. Whatever her reasons, my grandmother's refusal to move permanently to Newburgh left my mother with no alternative. If she was to continue to run the business as well as handle my father's estate, she would have to make a sacrifice. I would have to live at school during the week.

In September 1944, I returned to Mount Saint Mary's as a fourth-grader, but with a significant difference. Now I would be a boarder. I had attended the school since I was a four-year-old, so the environment was a familiar one to me. I suppose I should have been able to handle the separation from my mother, but it tore at me nonetheless. When the lights of our dormitory rooms were turned off by the nuns at night, I would cry myself to sleep, listening to the lonely whistle of the train making its way along the tracks close to the Hudson River. My father was gone, my mother had sent me away, and after my sun-filled former life, my future seemed dark and uncertain. I felt exiled, like Jane Eyre, orphaned and adrift. But of course, I wasn't really alone. Though at a distance, my mother was bent over the map of my life as she had spent years hunched over her beading frame. She was orchestrating my future the only way she knew how. It took me many years, but I eventually realized that it was at a great emotional cost that she sent me away at a time when she must have been at her loneliest.

The letters she wrote to my grandparents in Italy, which were saved and eventually given to me years later by an aunt, reveal something of the pain she hid from us.

> My heart is full of sorrow for the loss of my dear and unforgettable husband. As the time goes by I feel more lonely. I do not know how I can live without him.

> I live only for the dream that someday Dominick and I will be together again. I hope he is in God's glory with the beautiful Madonna. . . . The little Geraldine always says, "If my father was alive we would be very happy."

> I wish I too had died. The doctor told me I shouldn't work so hard, but the schools are very expensive and I want to carry out my husband's wishes.

Her resolve was firm. She was not going to allow my father's death to derail my education, as her father's illness had effectively done to hers. And I was going to be in as safe an environment as she could finance, an all-girls school supervised by nuns. She had already lost too many people she loved.

Seeing my mother's struggle, her family advised her to marry again. "You're too young, Antonetta," they told her. "You need a man to help you raise the children. Dominick wouldn't want you to be alone." But there was never another man for my mother; one husband was enough for her life. When an army major tried to court her at the end of the first year, she resisted. "You had one father," she told me, but what she really meant was that she had one husband. No one would ever replace the man she had waited so long to marry for love. And as I realized later, my mother was also very cautious about having another man in the house with me. The safety of her children meant everything.

As the months went by, her burdens grew increasingly difficult to handle. My father had left no insurance, and like other husbands of the period, he had kept his wife completely uninformed about money matters except for the five-and-dime, which was hers. In trying to protect her from financial worry, he had unwittingly placed her in an even more vulnerable position. He had also shielded her from the truth about his medical condition, never telling her that he was under a doctor's care for heart problems, never revealing that he had been taking medicine for high blood pressure. My mother wouldn't discover any of this until after his death, when she opened the little safe they kept in a closet. There was his medication, carefully hidden away. It now seems probable that my father's overprotection might actually have hastened his death. Instead of going straight to the hospital when he fell ill, he had the cabdriver bring him home, so as not to worry my mother. The tragic results of my father's well-intentioned paternalism made a lasting impression on me. I always made sure that I could take care of myself.

Finally, my mother had no recourse but to sell everything that had been so painstakingly accumulated in Newburgh—the house, the buildings on Mill Street, and the store.

"When you're a widow and you have to sell, you get nothing," she confided in me. It was a bitter loss, having to give up the last remnants of the life we had shared with my father. We moved back to New York City, this time to the South Bronx.

It was 1945. America was celebrating its hard-fought victory in World War II, and a renewed spirit of optimism was in the air. But the struggle was just beginning for the Ferraro family. In the space of a year, our family life underwent a dramatic change of scene. We moved from Newburgh to the South Bronx, from DuBois Street to Longfellow Avenue, from a spacious home to a small brownstone apartment.

I'll never forget the day I walked into the South Bronx apartment for the first time. Newburgh had spoiled me; I had grown accustomed to lawns and parks, and ferry rides across the Hudson. The South Bronx neighborhood, all brick and concrete, looked bleak—dirty and poor. Tucked away in boarding school, I had been insulated from the startling metamorphosis that was occurring in our lives, but I no longer had any choice. I had to face it now.

"What do you think?" my mother asked anxiously.

She had already completed the move; the small apartment was immaculate. The curtains were hung, and my beloved piano was polished and in place.

"It's so *small,*" I said, frowning.

My mother's face fell upon hearing my thoughtless words. But I was only ten years old, and it seemed as though my whole golden world had been destroyed. I think, in retrospect, my reaction was not that different from what any other child's would have been. Very simply, I wanted my father back. It wasn't so much the small rooms that distressed me as the fact that my towering father wouldn't be there to fill them.

In the Bronx, my mother became part of a community not unlike the one my grandmother had inhabited a generation before on Ninety-seventh Street. My aunt Jennie lived across the street with my cousin Joe, and her daughters Anita and Millie lived nearby with their families.

In spite of our drastically reduced circumstances, my mother was still viewed as the success, the designated family philanthropist. This was especially ironic, as she was the only sister apart from my aunt Jencie who had to hold a job outside the home. When my father was alive, he and my mother's three married brothers would each contribute money to my grandmother's support. The other two sons-in-law did not give any money, saying they couldn't afford it, and two of my aunts were widows and they were not expected to contribute. However, when my mother was widowed, my grandmother expected her to continue making a contribution to her support. With money very tight, my mother once told Maria Giuseppa that she couldn't afford it, and her mother was furious. She thought her daughter was lying and insisted that she continue her support. The persistent gleam of Antonetta's early prosperity blinded the family to the severity of her reduced circumstances. This had a great deal to do with the fact that Carl and I continued to receive the best educations. It was also because my mother was too proud to complain. This sustaining pride, a Corrieri trait she shared with my grandmother, had caused more than its share of problems before. Had my grandmother been able to humble herself and accept home relief after my grandfather's illness, my mother wouldn't have had to quit school and go to work at the age of fourteen.

My boarding school life, though I experienced it then as exile and emotional deprivation, turned out to be more beneficial than I could have realized at the time. Girls' schools offered terrific freedom—not liberty but of latitude. There were no restraints placed on achievement. I could be anything I wanted to be. But Mount Saint Mary's was not just any girls' school. It was a Catholic school, and that was a major consideration for my mother. The church taught that parents had an obligation to provide their children with a Catholic education. Every subject—science, civics, foreign languages—was taught through the prism of our faith. We were even advised what literature was appropriate: G. K. Chesterton was approved of; Ernest Hemingway was not. I was relieved to find that there was no church decree against Nancy Drew. I loved the teenage crime solver, who was smarter by far than her boyfriend and drove a snazzy red convertible to boot. Reading was my escape from loneliness. My favorite activity was to curl up in bed with a book.

At Mount Saint Mary's, we were encouraged to see ourselves as special, set apart by our Catholicism, and were constantly warned against dating non-Catholics, for fear that one of us could slip into the sure nightmare of a mixed marriage with a hell-bent outsider. Sequestered on one hand, encouraged to excel on another, I found in Mount Saint Mary's a haven, where my mother felt I could be safely kept while she carefully arranged my future life.

The Halloween after my father's death, I asked my mother if I could wear my brother Carl's old Uncle Sam costume. I was tired of being Miss America.

"Of course," she said. "It doesn't make any difference whether you're a boy or a girl. You can be whatever you want."

I was unaware at the time how potent—and unusual—such a statement was, especially from a woman who had received so little encouragement herself. My mother was forward thinking, an almost unconscious feminist before her time. She provided me with exactly the same opportunities as my brother. She used to say, "Remember, Gerry, your name is Ferraro. In Italian, *ferro* means iron. Iron bends, but it doesn't break. If things don't go the way you want, let it go, but never give up. Move on to the next thing." This wise advice would prove meaningful to me on many occasions in the years to come.

Whatever I accomplished throughout my life—making the smallest speech, or earning a Girl Scout badge—my mother was always the first to praise me. There was no resentment from her, no sense of competition. For my mother, everything I did was something she had not been able to do. This unwavering support came from a woman who labored from the moment she woke in the morning until she turned off her bedroom lamp at night.

She had taken the money from the sale of our family properties in Newburgh and made two investments. One was meant to provide us with income, and the other was to give us a vestige of the good life we had enjoyed before my father's death. She placed a down payment on a rustic cottage on Lake Hiawatha, New Jersey. The rest she invested in a small restaurant and bar she named Gerry's Place, located on the corner of Ninety-fourth Street and Second Avenue. She worked in the kitchen on the weekends and hired two of my uncles to run the place. Uncle Fred managed, and Uncle Mike bartended.

My mother's every moment was now consumed with one or another of her jobs. She beaded all day in a bridal shop, and then cooked weekend nights at Gerry's Place. Every evening during the week, in the spare room of the South Bronx apartment, she turned once again to her beading frame, resuming the painstaking work she thought she had left behind in the garment factory.

Several months into the sixth grade at Mount Saint Mary's, I suddenly became violently ill during the night. I was so sick that I couldn't even get out of my top bunk to get to the bathroom. I was too weak to call for help. By the morning, when Sister arrived in the dorm room to wake us, she discovered that I had been sick everywhere.

Sister was furious with me. She made me climb down from my bunk and take a shower. Then she had me wash my sheets by hand in the small bathroom sink. As I washed, I retched. By the time I had finished, I was barely able to stand. Weak with fever and shaking with chills, I was finally brought to the infirmary and put to bed. Then my mother was called.

When I woke later that day, my mother was standing beside me in the all-white room. She appeared to me like a rescuing angel, peering at me lovingly through the netted curtains that hung around the bed. The sisters hovered in the background, their black veils contrasting sharply with their pale faces.

This was the only harsh treatment I'd ever received at Mount Saint Mary's, but it was enough for my mother. She packed an overnight bag and took me home, intent on nursing me back to health herself.

As the cab pulled away from Mount Saint Mary's, I remember turning and looking back at the stone facade. It was the last time I would see it for fifty years.

Once at home, my mother immediately put me to bed and called the doctor. Since my only symptom was a sense of overwhelming nausea, he diagnosed my illness as a probable case of food poisoning. He assured my mother that I would be recovered within twenty-four hours.

When a week had passed and my nausea continued unabated, my mother panicked and called another doctor. He could find nothing wrong with me but suggested that I see a specialist. Dr. Goldfarb's office was a world away from the South Bronx—on Manhattan's tony Park Avenue. Undeterred by the prohibitive expense of consulting such a fancy doctor, my mother made an appointment.

Dr. Goldfarb diagnosed my problem as gastrointestinal upset, perhaps caused by the emotional trauma of the past few years. But he was most concerned by my blood count, which indicated that I was bordering on pernicious anemia.

My mother's questions were short and to the point.

"Can this be corrected?" she asked.

"Yes," the doctor said.

"What must be done?"

"Your daughter will need four iron injections a week, and an iron-rich diet."

I listened carefully as my mother began to negotiate a price for the treatments. Patients didn't normally dare to haggle, especially with doctors on Park Avenue. But this was on my behalf, and my mother wouldn't be denied. She was a force to contend with. The lessons I learned that day never left me. Without realizing it, she was preparing me for the give-and-take of a political career.

Dr. Goldfarb ultimately agreed to a reduced fee of $10 a week—a small fortune then—for two injections each visit. Even though this was what my mother paid for our monthly rent, she was grateful. Because of the seasonal nature of her work, she couldn't afford union dues, so we had no health insurance. She was instead forced to rely on her powers of persuasion and the kindness of doctors.

Even with the eight injections of iron each month, my recovery dragged. My grandmother came to stay with us for a while so someone would always be with me. When I was stronger, I would cross the street each day to my aunt Jennie's apartment, where I would wait for my mother to return from work and pick me up.

It didn't take me very long to adjust to my new surroundings in the South Bronx. Wherever my mother was quickly became home. Old enough at last to explore the neighborhood, I was sometimes allowed to attend a Saturday matinee with my new friends. Afterward, I would stop at the local bakery for a charlotte russe, a South Bronx delicacy. It was a moist cupcake stacked high with freshly whipped cream and topped with a bright red maraschino cherry. I began to more fully appreciate the benefits of living in the Bronx.

After I'd been home for a month, my mother began to grow concerned about my missing so much school. Whenever she mentioned my impending return to Mount Saint Mary's, I would burst into tears. I shuddered at the thought of having to face the nun who had made me wash my sheets. But more important, I didn't want to be without my mother anymore.

Finally, she went to the local parish, Saint John Chrysostom, to see if there was a spot for me in the sixth grade. She asked the priest whether he might waive at least part of the fee. She had already paid my nonrefundable tuition at Mount Saint Mary's. But the priest refused her request. He probably assumed that if she could afford to send me to a fancy boarding school, she could find a way to pay for a not-so-fancy parochial school in the South Bronx. The priest was right; somehow that's just what my mother did.

I loved my new life—attending the local school, taking piano lessons, walking home with my mother for lunch every day. As we listened to the serial drama *Stella Dallas* on the radio, she would cook me a chop or a hamburger to fight my anemia, contenting herself with a sandwich or an egg. She'd grown accustomed to listening to the radio soap operas during the relative ease of our old life in Newburgh, and she continued the habit in the South Bronx. The difference was that now her daily troubles rivaled those of the radio characters.

But this joyful interlude was brief. My mother knew that boarding school was the only way she could possibly continue the work schedule she had to maintain in order to continue to finance her children's education. Carl was ready to graduate from New York Military Academy and had already been accepted at Villanova College, where the bills for tuition, books, and room and board would tax my mother's already meager resources.

She took me with her when she traveled to Riverdale to ask her uncle Angelo for advice. In the space of thirty years he had risen from a pushcart vendor to a prosperous home owner and businessman. My mother had quietly noted the ascent of Angelo's children through their educational institutions. Angelo's oldest child, my cousin Fred, had toiled by his father's side, and he had gone on to graduate not only from college but from law school. Ann, Angelo's daughter, had attended Marymount College in nearby Tarrytown. On our visit we learned that there was also an elementary school at Marymount that accepted boarders. Cousin Ann offered my mother the telephone number of a Mother Catherine. The very next day my mother made an appointment.

It was the first of many trips the two of us would take on the Pelham Bay line to the 125th Street subway stop. We would then walk several blocks to the train station for the ride to Tarrytown. Crowning the top of a hill overlooking the Hudson River, Marymount's campus spread out regally from behind tall iron gates. I saw it for the first time with a sinking heart. To me it was more than just another boarding school. It marked another separation from my mother.

Mother Catherine greeted us, her face encircled by the crisp white coif that partially hid her stern features. She and my mother were the same age and height and they seemed to establish an immediate rapport—although they came from decidedly different backgrounds. Mother Catherine had been raised in a wealthy family, and her life was as centered on her religious order as my mother's was on her family.

As my mother discussed our financial situation with Mother Catherine, she mentioned some property that my father had left her in Italy, which had been rented out. This did nothing to add to our income, as there was then a prohibition against transferring any such monies to America.

Mother Catherine's face lit up.

"Could someone bring that money to Rome?" she asked my mother.

"Of course," my mother replied. "But what good would that do?"

Mother Catherine beamed. "Our motherhouse is in Rome, and we also have a school there," she told her. "We can take the money that's brought to Rome and count it against your daughter's board and tuition here."

My mother's eyes welled with tears, and she began to cry. God was opening a door for her, and He was doing it through this nun. By the time we got back on the train for the South Bronx, she was elated. Even in death, my father was reaching out to help us. All of the scrimping and praying would finally pay off. I was going to have the education that my parents had planned for me since the day I'd been born.

As my mother was the guiding beacon of my life, Mother Catherine was my navigator. She became my second mother, and on March 17, 1947, Marymount School became my second home. The nuns who ran Marymount belonged to the Religious of the Sacred Heart of Mary, an order which had been founded in France. It was a semicloistered community that ran girls' schools around the world. The nuns of this order were gentle, refined, well-educated teachers. They spent an enormous amount of their energies preparing us for academic excellence.

The majority of students at Marymount came from wealthy families, but it was an egalitarian community. We all wore identical navy blue uniforms and weren't allowed to use cash. I would return home to the South Bronx while my roommate returned to Fifth Avenue, but while we were at Marymount, we were all treated alike.

Here I would continue on the course my parents had intended for me prior to my father's death. My mother might be stirring pots of pasta and hoisting pizzas from a blazing oven, bending over her beading frame late at night, but her daughter was studying French. I was being taught the proper method for eating an artichoke as well as the correct way to "take leave of the queen"—that slow backing way from a regal presence that, to this day, I've yet to have the opportunity to use.

By the end of my first year, Mother Catherine told my mother that I had done so well on my final exams that I could skip the seventh grade and go directly into the eighth—if I could find a way to satisfy the seventh grade Latin requirement. My mother was not only proud of my academic achievement but, quite practically, thrilled at the prospect of saving a full year of tuition payments! Still, she didn't see how she could afford the cost of private Latin lessons.

Mother Catherine had the answer. The Sacred Heart sisters ran a camp in Sag Harbor, Long Island, called Cormaria. The camp accommodated twenty-four girls. Not only could they enjoy sports such as swimming and horseback riding, but academic help was available as well. Mother Catherine ran the camp herself and said she would be happy to teach me Latin. The tuition, she added, could again be paid through Rome.

I was happy with the plan, as long as I was able to spend the month of June with my mother and attend my brother's graduation from New York Military Academy. When he went off to Villanova in September, Carl would be the first of the Corrieri grandchildren to attend college. My mother's indomitable spirit had brought her halfway down the road to the nearly unreachable goal she had set—financing quality educations for both of her children.

I had the month of June to reacquaint myself with my South Bronx neighborhood. This was New York without air-conditioning, when people brought pillows out on their fire escapes to avoid the murderous heat that hung like a heavy drape in every apartment—as is still done in many inner-city neighborhoods. I was twelve, still young enough to play handball against garage walls and sit on the concrete stoops tossing jacks with my friends.

But there was no denying that one foot was already firmly planted in another, more sophisticated world. The sisters of the Sacred Heart taught us to be little ladies—in a manner totally foreign to the South Bronx. I still remember a particular June night, sitting on a high stool at Gerry's Place, waiting for my mother to be finished for the night. A woman from the neighborhood, a friend of my mother's, stopped by to say hello, and I jumped down from the stool and curtsied to her. She was flabbergasted.

Word of my polished sensibilities spread like wildfire, and I soon became a local curiosity. I was heralded as the cultured little girl from Longfellow Avenue.

I was home for only a month before setting off to Camp Cormaria for a summer of horseback riding, rowing boats, and total immersion in Latin. A pattern became established that would last throughout my school years. I was soon living away from home most of the time. Clad in school uniforms, with no particular past to identify me, I developed into a secure, distinctly American young woman, increasingly comfortable in the affluent worlds inhabited by my classmates. I became, in other words, exactly what my mother had always wanted me to be.

When I bought my first pair of jeans before leaving for camp, she made it clear that they were to be worn exclusively for horseback riding. She reminded me that only poor kids had to wear dungarees, and Antonetta Ferraro's daughter was not poor.

The thing I missed most during all of the years of striving and scrimping was the one thing my overworked mother was unable to provide me—more of herself.

She had by no means abandoned me to the sisters. She always appeared beautifully dressed at school events, and she was with me on all of the holidays. She also wrote to me regularly, and we always spoke on the phone twice a week. But I remained blithely unaware of the exact nature of her sacrifices; there was a significant part of her life that I was never allowed to see. She shielded me from the realities of her life just as my father had shielded her from his. Looking back now, this was a loss for both of us.

During the spring of my freshman year at Marymount, I found out they held an annual father-daughter dance. As soon as I heard about it, I requested permission to go home for the weekend. Even the thought of my father still brought a lump to my throat, and I wanted to avoid the painful spectacle of my schoolmates with their doting dads. But my request was denied. I was informed that this was a closed weekend, which meant that we were required to remain at school, although I was allowed to go off campus for part of the day.

My classmate Paula Giancola and I took the bus to White Plains and saw a matinee of *My Foolish Heart,* a film with Dana Andrews and Susan Hayward. It was a melodramatic war romance with a standard plot—a couple falls in love, gets married, and the bride becomes pregnant. The husband then goes off to war and is killed, leaving the wife a widow and their child without a father. Considering the circumstances of this particular weekend, the maudlin story line pierced any level of stoicism I'd been able to muster. All of the tears I'd held back since my father's death began to flow, and I was unable to stop crying. I wept so long and so hard that my friend Paula joined in with me. Returning to school, I remained inconsolable. Finally, my mother had to be called.

Once she had been fully apprised of the situation, she was livid when she conferred with the nuns. What was wrong with them? Why hadn't I been allowed to come home on such a difficult weekend?

"Your daughter must realize that her father is dead," the nun she spoke with replied tartly.

At this my mother exploded. "Realize that her father is dead? You don't think she knows? Why do you think my daughter lives at your school? Every day when she gets up and sees where she is, she knows her father is gone. Every night when she goes to her bed without a hug from her parents, she knows her father is dead." She exploded with a litany of everything that reminded us both of our loss. By the time she'd run out of steam, Marymount had a new policy. From that day on, girls who'd lost their fathers were permitted to go home on the weekend of the father-daughter dance. My mother had come to my defense and rescued me once again.

That year I asked my mother to show me how to bead. She sat me down at her frame, the four-sided fabric holder set on sawhorses, and handed me the needle. She stood by, patiently, watching me as I struggled to attach each bead, noting how slowly I worked and how clumsy I was. After about ten minutes, she reached over and took the needle out of my hand.

"Gerry," she said, "you'd better get an education or you'll starve to death."

While I was at Marymount I regularly attended Mass, and religious observance became an integral part of my life. Prayer and devotion were daily components of an atmosphere that was not only religious but spiritual. On retreat weekends, we spent our days in meditation and prayer, all observed in absolute silence. I began to look forward to these events. They gave me a great sense of peace, spiritual comfort, and a calm detachment from the pressures of the outside world. This was all new to me. My grandmother's devotion to religion had been based on ancient southern Italian fears, reverence for powers beyond the scope of the church. There were many elements of superstition attached to the worship of the Christian God, including the power of the evil eye. My mother's practice of religion was also tinged with an Old World sensibility. It was centered on rosary beads, votive candles, holy cards, and novenas. But at Marymount, a different, more intellectual focus was encouraged, one grounded in theological awareness as much as blind emotional faith.

In those years, many young Catholic women were entering convents, and schools like Marymount were the primary breeding grounds for the religious orders. Becoming a nun was a way for a young woman to pursue an intellectual and spiritual life without the interference and pressures of marriage and motherhood. In spite of the rigid rules and practices attached to religious life, there was a freedom there that neither my mother nor hers had ever realized. Since the convent and novitiate where the young nuns trained were on the same grounds as the school, it was impossible not to be aware of the new group of postulants that were everywhere when I returned at the end of each summer. In their black dresses, short veils, and still-unshorn hair, these were often girls not much older than I. Yet already they were cloaked in mysteries, as if they'd discovered a secret that the rest of us could not know.

Studious and bright, I was conscious of the restricted roles that my mother and grandmother had been permitted to play, and I knew I wanted more than they'd been allowed. I was attracted to a life beyond that of a wife and mother, and I wasn't averse to the possibility of a religious life. Its potential shimmered brightly before me throughout my years at Marymount.

By my final year of high school, the senior-class mistress, Mother Marguerite, had begun talking with me regularly about the possibility of becoming a nun. Even though I wanted to go to college and become a writer, I saw joining the order as a distinct possibility. I dreaded the thought of having to leave the haven that had allowed me to excel and sheltered me since the uncertainty and illness that followed the death of my father.

But I soon began to feel pressured into making a decision. When I finally confessed my uncertainty to my mother, she called Mother Marguerite and told her that I was too young to make such a choice at this point in my life. I had been raised in a convent and had no other experience. How could I make an informed decision? If in two years, at the age of eighteen, I chose a religious path, she said it would be fine with her. This is what my mother told Mother Marguerite, but I think it was just a delaying tactic, intended to gain her time to orchestrate the next stage of my life. My mother thought that being a nun was fine for other people, but she had no intention of giving her only daughter to a semicloistered religious community. She had been drawing the blueprints for my life, and had grander plans than that in mind. Antonetta Ferraro's daughter was going to college. That decision had been made when I was a little girl, and her resolve had been strengthened only a few weeks earlier during a visit to my grandmother. As usual, Carl and I had been the center of discussion, and my mother was talking about her hope that I would win a scholarship to college. My uncle Tom, the same man who had so carelessly put a lid on my mother's education so many years before, now offered his studied opinion on me. "Why bother, Antonetta? Gerry's pretty. She'll get married."

My mother understood exactly what Tom was saying. She stared at him with gleaming eyes, glad for the opportunity to speak back. "You're right, my Gerry is a beauty," she said. "But when you educate a boy, you educate a boy alone. When you educate a girl, you educate a family."

And that's exactly what my mother planned to do. She was going to educate a family.

My mother wasn't a great businesswoman. In fact, her financial skills were so negligible that she forever rushed from one job to the next to keep us afloat. The cabin at Lake Hiawatha had been sold long ago. The money was invested in some land in Lake Hopatcong, with the hope that someday we would build a house on it, somehow, someway. One day it was foreclosed. The restaurant, Gerry's Place, barely managed to pay for itself. Even though she had put up all of the money to purchase the place in return for Uncle Fred's commitment to manage it, she saw little profit at the end of each month. This was more of a problem for my mother than for Fred. He somehow managed to drive a Cadillac, buy his wife a mink coat, and vacation in Havana. Whenever my mother asked my uncle about his accounting, he patiently explained that he had to pay off the cops on the beat. He claimed that if they weren't taken care of, they would come up with phony excuses to close the place down and run them out of business.

Remembering my father's bitter experiences with the state liquor authority in Newburgh, my mother found Uncle Fred's explanations plausible. And it turned out that Fred was likely telling the truth. Several years later, the Knapp Commission found that many small business owners in New York were regularly paying off cops in order to stay in business.

But never a word was mentioned about these troubles to my brother, Carl, or me. Years later, she admitted to me, "My pillow knew how unhappy I was. What good was it to tell my children?"

It was only on rare occasions that my mother's veneer appeared to crack and I was allowed a glimpse at the battle she continuously fought in order to provide us with a better life.

It was Christmas Eve 1949 in the South Bronx. Full of French, field hockey, and fancy manners, I was home for the holidays, waiting for my mother. She was late returning from work. We were going to go out together to buy some last-minute gifts and our tree, which was always much cheaper if it was purchased the night before Christmas. When she finally arrived, we rushed out to Southern Boulevard, but we had to stop at the Woolworth counter. She hadn't eaten all day. When she finished her slice of pound cake and cup of coffee, she reached for her purse to remove her pay envelope. It was gone. Flushed and distraught, we rushed over to the police station on Simpson Street, where the desk officer shrugged nonchalantly. "That's a shame, lady, but what do you want us to do? It's Christmas Eve."

It was disturbing to see my mother so vulnerable. Her purse could be snatched without consequence. A policeman could dismiss her pleas for help. She somehow managed to salvage our Christmas by means that were never entirely clear—perhaps she hocked one of the few pieces of jewelry my father had given her. Whatever the harsh reality, she made sure that when I returned to school, it was with fine memories of a wonderful holiday spent with my mother.

It seems ironic that the education my mother struggled to provide me with took me ever further from her world. There was a price to be paid for growing up in one culture and gaining admittance to another. There were times when I wasn't quite sure where I belonged. At school, I was the editor of the newspaper, the copy editor of the yearbook, captain of the intramural team. I was the basketball and softball player, the girl who made up a boyfriend just so she could have an excuse to knit argyle socks, which I then gave to my brother. But when I returned home to the South Bronx, I was just Gerry, the daughter of frugal, exhausted Antonetta Ferraro. Even though my mother assured me that one day I'd have a maid, she still made sure I knew how to cook, clean, sew, iron clothes, and wash windows.

But it wasn't until my junior year, when I invited my roommate Christina Bakker home for the weekend, that I realized how conflicted I'd become. As we got off the subway, I found myself changing the normal route I took to our apartment so we could avoid the ugly garages that lined Whitlock Avenue. With a sharp pang of guilt, I realized that I was embarrassed by where I lived. My mother was so thrilled by Christina's visit that she was oblivious to my turmoil. But throughout Christina's stay with us, I agonized at the smallness of our apartment, the plainness of our surroundings. I was ashamed of where I came from, and I never invited a schoolmate home again.

Marymount had exposed me to a world of privilege. I mingled with the daughters of movie stars and business leaders. One of my friends was Patsy Busch, whose parents owned a chain of jewelry stores. When I went to a birthday party at her house, it was like stepping into another world. We were served by a maid, and spent the day playing croquet on the spacious, manicured lawn of the grand Busch estate. I wasn't completely unaware of how my mother would view all of this. I was savoring it through her eyes, storing up every detail so that I could tell her about it later.

Patsy didn't quite fit the mold of a wealthy heiress. She was always in trouble with the nuns for transgressing one rule or another. She would put makeup on her legs, hoping they wouldn't notice she wasn't wearing stockings. (They did, of course.) She chewed gum and lost her "excellence," which meant she couldn't go home for the weekends. And when she was allowed to go to Tarrytown for the day, invariably someone would report that she had been smoking.

When Patsy graduated from high school, she did another surprising thing. She joined the convent. I guess she got that rebellious streak out of her system, although to this day, after forty-five years as a religious, she still has a wicked twinkle in her eye, and I love seeing her.

As the years passed at Marymount, I grew increasingly confident. By my senior year, when one of the sisters asked if I would remain at school for the father-daughter dance and serve as a hostess, I readily agreed. Somehow I knew it was time. Finally, at the age of sixteen, I was able to stand at the entrance and greet all of the fathers, though none of them was mine.

When I began at Marymount, my mother always accompanied me on my trips back to Tarrytown, but as I grew older I prevailed upon her to let me travel alone. She still insisted on going with me to the

125th Street station and waiting until the train departed. I always took a seat by the window, and we both waved until we couldn't see each other anymore. Only then would my mother turn away and head back to her life of solitude. She was more isolated than I could have imagined, a blue-collar widow of the 1950s, her world revolving around her work, her family her only social life. After she died, I found yellowed newspaper clippings she must have kept for solace. Among them were *A Prayer for Those Who Live Alone; When Loneliness Is New;* and *For Those Who Lose a Child.* When I read them, I wept.

I don't think I ever fully realized how difficult it must have been for her to enter the rarefied world of Marymount on those special school occasions. Other mothers came through the gates in fancy new cars, accompanied by their husbands. But my mother always arrived alone in a cab and, much to my consternation, was usually late.

But whenever she did arrive, she always looked wonderful, dressed in a tailored suit, her hair beautifully coiffed and swept away from her face. It dawned on me years later that she might have been working until the last minute to pay for her train ticket, or perhaps she purposefully arrived late so that she could limit the time she had to socialize. She was never comfortable mingling with other parents. Fresh from the kitchen of Gerry's Place or the back room of the bridal shop, what did she have in common with movie stars and wealthy businessmen?

She wore a beautiful white suit for my high school graduation, a day that was the culmination of so many dreams. Although the audience was filled with luminaries, including the handsome young junior senator from Massachusetts, John F. Kennedy, who was there to see his cousin Ann Gargan graduate, my mother had eyes only for me. She beamed as I rose to deliver one of the graduation speeches and was awarded a full-tuition scholarship to Marymount College. As I stood on the stage before the assembled dignitaries and accepted this honor, I looked out and found my mother's eyes. It had taken three generations for a woman in my family to reach this crossroads. But I held no illusions. I hadn't accomplished it alone. My mother and I had done it together.

• FIVE •

COMING HOME

Just at the time of life when many young people are leaving their families to go off to college, I was finally able to return home. My mother was lonely, and I was tired of living without her. After my high school graduation and nearly a decade of separation, we were reunited again.

Somehow my mother had been able to perform an almost magical act, shielding me from the realities of her life. Everything had always been lovely when viewed from train windows and at special events. But once I moved back home, my mother finally came into sharp focus. Part of me had always understood that she'd had a rough time since my father's death. What I hadn't realized was how poorly she'd been taking care of herself. She slept irregularly and often skipped meals, eating meat only once or twice a week because of the cost. She had put off going to the dentist for so long that her teeth eventually had to be pulled for dentures, a great source of embarrassment to her. She no longer worked in the kitchen at Gerry's Place. Instead she was bent over her beading frame full-time. She never took a single day off, even when she was ill. She had her shoes resoled and often wore my cast-off skirts and sweaters. She'd always made such a fine showing at Marymount, in her Persian lamb coat and fancy hats that my father had bought her years before. I was shocked both by her fragility and the tough, frugal quality of her life. She seemed so unnecessarily hard on herself that it hurt me to see it.

I was also confused about my mother's relationship with her family. Never hesitant to ask for my mother's help, to lean on her and take from her, the relatives seemed to be unaware of her isolation. In my memory and imagination, our Italian family was knit together as one; when I was younger my cousins might as well have been siblings—that's how close we were. I could not fathom how this distance had grown between my mother and everyone else. And she never spoke of it.

I think, looking back, that her isolation was in part self-imposed. She was so strong, so unyielding. Even as a young girl she had set her iron will against convention. She had married late and well. She had asked for support only once, when she begged her mother to come to Newburgh after my father's death. My grandmother's refusal sealed the resolve in my mother's heart, and she never asked for help again.

After I was home for a while, a subtle switch occurred, and I became increasingly protective of my mother, especially when I saw how her family treated her. I remember one incident with bright clarity. Soon after I'd moved back, we attended a wedding. After the reception, I watched in amazement as our relatives simply got into their cars and pulled away, leaving us stranded. None of our family had thought to ask us how we were getting home, and my mother was too proud to request a ride, afraid that it might inconvenience someone. She had for so long been the rock that others leaned on, it never dawned on any of her family that she might need some support herself—and she wasn't about to ask.

I began to stand up for my mother with both sides of our family. When my uncle Dominick, my father's younger brother, made a critical comment about her, I lit into him, retorting that he had long ago ceded any right to criticize my mother for anything. He'd only bothered with us when my father was alive, but had washed his hands of us and disappeared after his death. After that imbroglio, he and everyone else in the family watched what they said about my mother—at least in front of me.

I had graduated from high school as a star. I was an award winner, a scholar, an athlete, an all-American girl of the 1950s. I was accustomed to success and comfortable with the trappings of achievement. Living with my mother opened my eyes. I saw for myself how narrow her world was, how bland her constant diet of self-sacrifice. There was no room in her life to savor her intellect, to read a book, enjoy a play, or to go to the opera. Instead, her days were filled with graduated levels of work and worry. My mother was fixated on my brother Carl. He had been drafted in 1950 and sent to Germany after completing his third year at Villanova, and my mother was terrified of losing him, her only boy, her last surviving son. All of her hopes for the future rested on my brother and me. Sensing the fervor of her resolve made me want to succeed all the more. And when I caught an occasional glimpse of the aching sadness she carried for those she had lost, I longed to be all things to her so she wouldn't grieve.

My mother, I saw, lived with ghosts—those of her dead children and her husband. I regretted that I had never known the young, bright Antonetta before she was scarred by so many tragedies—the girl who loved to dance and laugh, the girl so picky about her beaux. She was probably more like me than I would have imagined. Had she been allowed to continue her schooling, who knows what she might have achieved?

For the most part, my mother hid her private sorrows. There was only one occasion when she allowed the tears to flow with abandon, and that was October 13, the anniversary of Gerard's death. Over the years, if I was home on those days, I tiptoed around her and tried to respect the sanctity of her grief. But the first year I moved back, the ritual came to an abrupt halt.

On that particular October 13, I was running down the sidewalk because I was late for school, and a car suddenly backed out of a garage and knocked me down. I wasn't hurt, but I was shaken and dizzy. I brushed myself off and rushed to school, where I arrived five minutes late. My professor, Dr. Clancy, was a stickler about time. "You're five minutes late," he growled. "That will be a half cut."

Breathless and flushed, I stared at him in disbelief. Then I got mad. "I'll tell you what," I snapped. "Make it a full cut." And I stormed out of the room.

My mother was alarmed to see me returning to the apartment as she was getting ready to leave, and when I told her about being knocked down by a car, she broke into a fresh wave of sobs. "Oh, God is punishing me, God is punishing me," she cried.

"What do you mean?" I asked. She was totally beside herself.

"All these years I've cried for Gerard, and God isn't happy with me because I am not thinking of my living children."

That was the most ludicrous thing I had ever heard, but my mother refused to be consoled. She said, "I will never shed another tear for your brother. He is in God's hands." In this way, my mother bargained with God to insure my safety.

I had always wanted to go to college at Barnard or Columbia, where I intended to study journalism, to become a newspaper reporter. I loved to write, and one of my youthful heroines had been Nellie Bly, the first truly daring female foreign correspondent. However, as the time for college applications had neared, my ambitions had been forced to undergo some adjustment. The nuns hadn't permitted application to a non-Catholic college, and we couldn't have afforded one in any case. Instead, I received a scholarship to Marymount College in Tarrytown, which I transferred to Seventy-first Street in Manhattan, closely affiliated with the Tarrytown branch.

In September 1952, I entered a class of ninety-one students at Marymount, the largest ever admitted. Marymount had long held a reputation for graduating wealthy girls, with most degrees quickly followed by a Mrs., but that year there was an unusually high number of scholarship students, and I was one of them.

My mother ground away at my vocational aspirations by asking me two questions again and again: How many women got jobs as reporters on newspapers? How much did those jobs pay? The answers to both of those questions were not exactly confidence inspiring. Journalism was still an almost entirely male profession. There were few women making it at that time, and if they were working, they were paid considerably less than men. Those weren't my mother's only questions. "Suppose you get married and stop working, then your husband dies?" she asked, with the voice of experience. "Is being a reporter a job you can go back to after you've been away from it for years?"

It was clear that she was filtering the possibilities of my future through the perspective of her own past. We began to talk about other jobs I might be interested in doing—becoming a teacher, for example. It was a guaranteed, stable, respected profession. It was relatively well paying. It was also the kind of work my mother probably would have chosen if she'd had the chance. So we decided together. Although I'd begun college as an English major with a journalism minor, I switched my minor to education.

Since I'd skipped a grade in high school, I was younger than the other girls in my freshman class. This had always made me feel a little out of place in high school, and I was now determined to play catch-up and fit in. I quickly fell in with the hippest kids in school. I even asked my mother to teach me how to smoke so I'd look older. I remember my first cigarette vividly. I puffed, got dizzy, lay down, and then tried again. Eventually I got the hang of it. It was more like *it* got a hang on *me,* as I only had to assert even more effort later on, when I decided to kick the habit.

Marymount offered an excellent liberal arts education within a strong Catholic context. It was a familiar and comfortable extension of my high school years—the same order of nuns, the supportive all-girls environment. I did well there, excelling on the debating team and becoming an editor of the school newspaper. Since the school offered no education courses in teaching methods, I was able to pick those up at Hunter College, located just a few blocks away. The faculty worked hard to broaden the horizons of the scholarship students, many of whom were the daughters of immigrant or first-generation Irish Americans and Italian Americans. We were strongly encouraged to assimilate, move out into the mainstream, to behave as both intellectuals and modern young women.

In this respect, my grandmother Maria Giuseppa and I became separated by a wider chasm than that of years. Women of my grandmother's generation fought assimilation with every bone in their bodies. They made whatever accommodations were necessary to maintain the language and customs of their homeland. My grandmother saw American ways as more frivolous than white bread, and dangerous to the survival of the family. She was a strong woman, but she believed there was value in being deferential. In photographs taken of my grandmother, her eyes were always cast downward.

My mother's generation—those who were born in America—was nearly ripped in two by the stress of trying to hold the old and the new in balance. In many important ways, my mother was ahead of her times, but in others she was conflicted. She adored me, and she wanted every opportunity for me, but I frightened her a bit with my breezy style, my inquiring mind, and my refusal to defer to men or custom. She worried that I would make foolish choices and stray along dangerous paths.

I, of course, saw none of this. Like all young people, I lived in the moment and dreamed of the future. The past held no consequence. Maria Giuseppa's life of deferring and sacrifice was as foreign to me as the remote hillside of her birth.

My adjustment to college life was terrific—if my social life the first year isn't factored in. It was nonexistent. My mother insisted that I was still too young to date. This was the only area where she treated me differently from Carl. He had been allowed to date earlier, stay out later, and go off to visit friends. The most social life my mother would allow me was attending Catholic War Veterans meetings with my cousin Joe from across the street. I spent my first year of college churning internally against the sudden appearance of Old World barriers.

This experience was heightened by the arrival of my grandmother, who lived with us for a few months after her youngest son, Mike, got married and moved out of the apartment on Ninety-seventh Street. My grandmother was a powerful figure in our family, but I had spent very little time around her when I was growing up, and she was a mystery to me. I knew that she had emigrated from Italy at a young age, but it wouldn't be until much later that I would learn the full story of her voyage, the death of her aunt, and her fated marriage to my grandfather. In large part, the distance between my grandmother and me was due to language. My grandmother always spoke Italian, and she claimed that she could neither speak nor understand more than a few words of English—although she always seemed to know exactly what I was saying. God only knows what she thought of me—the all-American girl in poodle skirts and bobby socks. She mostly kept it to herself, although some of my habits astonished her.

I was a night person, not a morning person. I had carefully calculated down to the minute how much time it took me to get ready and off to school, and I set my alarm for as late as I could, to eke out every last second of sleep. Having been raised in a boarding school, I had perfected a lightning-fast routine, and this served me well.

The first morning after my grandmother arrived, I jumped out of bed, raced to the bathroom, and found that the door was closed. My grandmother was in there. I pounded on the door—a rude thing to do, but I was desperate and she was hard of hearing. From that morning on, my grandmother and I worked around my schedule. And she marveled at my speed. She once said, "Everybody else gets dressed in one-two-three. Gerry, she gets dressed in *one.*"

That first summer, I went to work at an accounting firm on Forty-second Street run by two brothers. The firm employed several women as typists, and that was my job, but my boss wanted me also to learn shorthand. He paid for me to attend a course, but I never got the hang of it.

My boss was always hovering, and he made me uncomfortable. Often he would stand very close to me, jiggling the change in his pocket as I typed. I would deliberately make mistakes and say very sweetly that it was because I got a little nervous being watched. He would then move away. This process would repeat itself constantly. Sometimes he would finger the edges of his waxed mustache and tell me how pretty I was. It was sickening. I would have quit, but I needed the money. I never told my mother about him because she wouldn't have let me stay.

When Christmas came, my boss called each of the typists into his office, one at a time, for our Christmas bonuses. As the other women came out, they told me what they had received. One of them, who was full-time, got $15, and I hoped I would as well. When I went into the office, he stood up to hand me my envelope. As he did, he moved toward me to kiss me. I backed up, took the envelope with my left hand, opened the door behind me with my right, and said, "Thank you, and I quit." My envelope contained $25! Eight years later when I was collecting affidavits from former employers that I needed in order to be admitted to the bar, I called and asked my former boss to send me one. He insisted I come and pick it up personally. I was married, pregnant, and probably not as fast on my feet, so I sent my husband, John, to get it.

At the end of my freshman year at Marymount, my mother and I moved to a two-family house in a residential neighborhood of Astoria, Queens. The house stood in the shadow of the Triborough Bridge. Our new apartment was small, and it was also close to the noisy elevated train, but the area was safer and it was familiar ground for my mother, who had spent her years as a bride a few blocks away. Back then she had owned a home and had a husband, a car, and a business. Now she was a widow of many years, working as a crochet beader. If the thought ever occurred to her, if she ever held up the past and present for comparison, she never said so. In this, as in all matters, she was without bitterness or complaint.

The apartment was small, but it was all we needed, since Carl had recently been discharged from the army and was living in Italy. Though he had been drafted at the end of his junior year at Villanova and had never received his degree, he was still able to get accepted into medical school at the University of Bologna. My mother was thrilled.

Our new apartment in Astoria also brought us within fortuitous proximity of my cousin Nick Ferraro and his family, with whom I grew close. Later a judge and the Queens district attorney, Nick was the one who eventually gave me a start in Queens politics.

When I turned nineteen, my mother relaxed her strict regulations about dating. I was allowed to go out, although I had to bring my dates back to the apartment at the end of the evening so my mother could look them over and, of course, feed them. I put up with these late-night socials, although I think my mother enjoyed the company. She seemed happy standing at the stove, frying batches of pizza dough and serving them piping hot to my hungry suitors. The boys I dated never objected to coming upstairs. In fact, they seemed to look forward to it.

My mother tried to be discreet in voicing her opinions about my dates, but sometimes she couldn't resist making a comment. One medical student I had been seeing was a great dancer and a nice person, but he was not particularly good looking and he had enormous ears. After one of what she decided were too many dates, my mother said to me one afternoon, "You know, Gerry, if you marry him, traveling on your honeymoon will be easy."

"Easy? Why?" I innocently asked.

"With his ears, you can jump on his back and he'll fly you wherever you want to go." We both collapsed with laughter. That was the end of the medical student.

Once I was allowed to begin dating, I quickly became popular. The phone rang so frequently that my mother grew suspicious. "So many boys are calling. What are you doing that so many guys are asking you out?" she asked me, her eyebrow arched expectantly, her hands on her hips.

"Nothing," I retorted. I was insulted, and it was true. The furthest I allowed a boy to go was to kiss me. Unlike my mother's generation, mine felt that we should be allowed to meet more people and play the field. We went out with many boys, but not seriously, and we were not sexually promiscuous. We were too scared, for one thing. As a Catholic-reared and -educated young woman, I figured that if God didn't get me, my mother surely would.

I met John Zaccaro, the man I would marry, by chance. At the time, I had been dating several college men, one of whom was named Vinnie Lionetti. One night we went with a group to a club in Greenwich Village. One of the other young men who joined us that night was John, who was there with a date. John was already a senior at Iona, a darkly handsome young man with soft brown eyes, curly hair, and a slight gap between his front teeth when he smiled. He had a soft-spoken manner and a dry sense of humor that I found appealing. From that time on, John and his dates would sometimes double-date with Vinnie and me. John and I became friends, and I recognized a spark in those brown eyes when he looked at me. I liked him, too, but for the time being that's as far as it went.

During those years, my mother and I operated as a team, unified against a difficult world. Even when I was busy with my social life and eventual student teaching at Hunter College Elementary School, we were still there for each other totally. We called each other "dirlfriend," a silly endearment that signified our closeness. While my friends were putting more distance between themselves and their mothers, I was reveling in having her as a companion. I trusted her completely and could not imagine being without her. Together we did what we could to make ends meet. Once my mother and I shared a job at Loft's, a candy store chain that sold boxed and loose candy. We'd split the evening shift at the store on Ditmars Boulevard, which was within walking distance of our apartment.

When my classmate Mary Ann LoPresti asked if my mother and I would consider moving into the apartment above a doctor's office near her home, with free rent in exchange for cleaning the office, we jumped at the opportunity. Dr. Kroll, a colleague of Mary Ann's father, was a radiologist, and the apartment above his office was twice the size of our current one. Every night after the office closed, my mother and I would go down together and empty the wastebaskets, then straighten up the examining rooms, the staff kitchen, and the bathroom. It was easy work, and the apartment was the best place we'd lived since Newburgh.

* * *

After her brief stay with us, my grandmother returned to the apartment on Ninety-seventh Street, where she had spent most of her adult life. It was there that she collapsed the year before my graduation, suffering a stroke as she was cleaning the insides of her windows. It was somehow appropriate that my rigorously immaculate grandmother died with a cleaning rag in her hand. And it was a blessing that she was taken quickly, with her dignity intact. Maria Giuseppa was eighty when she died, but still beautiful, with pristine white hair and a sweet, girlish purity in her face. At the time of her death she had three living daughters, including my mother, and their emotional outbursts at her funeral were like operatic arias—one seemed to outdo the other.

When the service was over, we made our way in a caravan to the cemetery. I stood beside my mother, sober and reverent, although I was unable to fully experience the intensity of grief that was being displayed around me. During the service I had found my thoughts straying to the only other funeral of significance I had ever attended—that of my father. The recollection of his death brought a watery glaze to my eyes. I wept for my grandmother through the memory of my father.

Just as my grandmother's coffin was being lowered into the grave, my mother gave a small shudder and fainted dead away. My cousin Teresa and I carried her back to the car and got her into the backseat. At that point, our aunt Anna, who could never bear to be outdone by my mother, followed suit, and she was carried away from the grave. Our aunt Jennie, as small as she was wide, watched her two sisters go down and began to teeter. When her burly sons grabbed hold of her and awkwardly tried to carry her toward the distant cars, one holding each of her arms and the other each of her legs, something just let go inside me. I looked at Teresa and we both collapsed in fits of laughter. The tears ran down our faces. With that display, my mother was able to revive herself enough to reprimand us both. She was furious at what she saw as our lack of respect. I hadn't any intention of being callous. I was reacting to a display of hysteria. But it was true that I was too young to fully understand that a unique era had come to an end with the death of my grandmother.

By my senior year of college I was dating John Zaccaro. He had graduated from Iona with a commission in the Marine Corps. John's quiet, agreeable way was a good counterbalance to my energetic personality. He was also from a well-established Italian family. My mother never made an issue of the nationalities of the different boys I dated, but she had a definite soft spot for John. I sometimes thought he must have reminded her of another courteous young Italian, one who had charmed her years ago. More than anything else, my mother wanted to make certain that I was settled. She wanted to know that if something happened to her, I would have a husband to take care of me and a stable job to fall back on. She had been so strained by the loss of my father and her own resulting financial insecurity that she was determined the same thing would not happen to me. In the warm eyes of John Zaccaro she glimpsed my safe and happy future. And in this, as in so many other matters, her instinct was correct.

The day of my graduation from college, my mother threw a party for me at our apartment. There was a brand-new white 1956 Buick convertible with red upholstery parked out front. This was my mother's graduation gift to me. She had made the down payment of $400, and I would be taking over the monthly payments. I was now a licensed teacher, having recently passed the city exam. I was also the first woman in our family to receive a college degree. Radiant in new dresses, my mother and I floated among friends and family, the new car as shining as our hopes. By now we had both grown expert in the art of frugal embellishment; no one could have guessed how little money we had between us.

I was twenty years old when I received my teaching degree, but I wasn't ready to finish my own education. I enjoyed student teaching, but I was also eager to continue my studies. I thought about going for a master's in education or English, but I eventually decided to go to law school. The interview with the admissions office at Fordham University culminated with the comment, "I hope you're serious, Gerry. You're taking a man's place, you know." But I was undaunted, and my mother was thrilled by my decision; she told me she had always been impressed by Portia's portrayal of a lawyer in Shakespeare's *The Merchant of Venice*. In fact, she could still recite the speech she had learned at P.S. 150, as if she herself were standing in a courtroom: "The quality of mercy is not strained . . . ," she would begin. I was impressed that the schools were so advanced in my mother's youth that the children learned Shakespeare before eighth grade graduation. Later, it occurred to me that in classes where some children spoke English and others did not, Shakespeare, with its foreign-sounding dialogues, was tantamount to a third language that all could share.

It was while I was attending law school that I first joined a local political club. During the political season, I would stop on the way home from class at night and do the grunt work of stuffing envelopes for local candidates. I wasn't unusual. Many law students did the same thing in the hope that it might lead to a position after graduation. Jobs in law firms were scarce, especially if you were Catholic, attending night school, and female.

I was an impatient young woman, and I easily grew bored, but the campaign work always held my interest. I liked the tension, fever, and unpredictability of politics. There was something about it that excited me on a very deep level.

• SIX •

A Place of My Own

By day I was a schoolteacher and by night a law student. I had very little time to spend with my mother. Occasionally I would catch her with a wistful look on her face, and when I asked her what she was thinking, she'd sigh a little and say, "Oh, your brother. It's been so long since I saw my Carl."

Carl was still living in Bologna, attending school. But he would often travel south to visit with our aunts and uncles, staying in the house in Marcianise where our father was raised. Our mother had given him access to money from our rental properties there while he went to school. I knew she missed him desperately. Carl was a shining star in her eyes, her only living son. I always thought that she loved Carl more than me, but it wasn't true. Carl, with his charming personality and bright mind, had been the center of her life long before I was born. And as he reached adulthood, he looked more and more like our father. My mother prayed that Carl would eventually settle down in America so she could have both her children with her. But Carl had wanderlust in him, something my mother had a hard time understanding. It puzzled her that he chose to live in Italy. This was the country whose narrow promise her parents and her husband had left behind for what they saw as better opportunities in America.

I had been thinking of my father's homeland myself. I wanted to visit Marcianise, to meet my father's family, to touch a little of what I had missed of him when I was growing up. When I approached my mother about the idea of our taking a trip together to Italy, she couldn't imagine how we would afford it. We were always scraping to get by. I had figured it out. I went to Chase Manhattan Bank and got my first loan, in the amount of $1,200. It would cover our bills for the summer and our transportation over. While we were in Italy, we wouldn't need to spend anything. We could live on the money generated from my father's rental properties, and we could also use that money for our return trip home.

So the trip was arranged. I asked my friend Mary Ann LoPresti if she wanted to come along, and since her aunt was going to be there for the summer, it was perfect for her. My mother refused to fly—as she continued to do her entire life—so we set sail on the SS *Constitution*. The trip over was a lot of fun. I was in a constant state of delight. It warmed my heart to see my mother so happy. She had left her bundle of cares behind at the dock in New York and was far more relaxed than I'd seen her in years. She regaled us with stories of her first trip to Italy with my father, and she marveled that the sickly little Carl of that long-ago visit had grown into such a strapping young man. As the SS *Constitution* approached the beautiful harbor at Naples, my mother and I stood on the deck with our arms around each other and lifted our faces into the warm Mediterranean breeze. I gazed, astounded, at the most beautiful sight I had ever seen—the water so blue it might have been painted; the hills dotted with houses; Mount Vesuvius rising up majestically in the distance. I imagined my father looking back at this vision as he said good-bye to his native land and set sail for America thirty-seven years before, and I wondered how anyone could leave a place of such beauty. But even as I wondered, I knew. Destiny transcends beauty. What my father sought was something more.

Carl was waiting for us at the dock, and my mother cried with joy at the sight of him. We piled in his car and headed north to Marcianise.

Remembering my father's love for the town of his birth, I was eager to see it—and unimpressed when I did. A typical small town, with very narrow roads and alleyways through which we could barely squeeze a car, it was not the magnificent place I always imagined it to be. I had an American girl's notion of wealth, and this small place set among fields of cannabis was not my picture of prosperity.

The house where Don Carlo and Maria Alessandra Ferraro raised their family was located on a narrow street. The building was very old and looked run down. On the ground floor in front was a butcher shop, which produced an unappealing odor. My grandfather had died in 1948; my grandmother in 1950. Two years later the space where Don Carlo had his office was rented to the butcher. His wife, with rosy cheeks to match her bloodstained apron, came to the door to greet us.

Everything about the place intrigued me—from the crumbling facade to the narrow balcony that ran the length of the building. This had been my father's home, and touching these walls meant touching him.

I particularly loved a lovely stone archway that led into a small courtyard where two orange trees and two lemon trees grew. I could easily imagine my sociable father entertaining his friends here.

My brother showed us around the house and other land in a proprietary manner, as if it were his own. I was soon to discover that he believed it was. My mother and I hadn't brought very much money with us, expecting to have access to the income from the rentals. But

Carl doled out each *lira* resentfully, and in meager spurts. He made us feel as if we were robbing him, and I was furious about it. To treat my mother with such disrespect! But my mother shrugged it off. She refused to utter a word of criticism against Carl. Was she afraid she'd lose him if she questioned his behavior? Did she defer to him as the man of the family, as she'd been raised to do? I didn't know, but it had always been this way.

We were in Italy, and I was eager to see the sights and get a feeling for the country. Carl turned out to be a reluctant tour guide, but one day I insisted that he show us the country. "I didn't come here to just sit around and look at you," I told him. So my mother and I got into Carl's car for a trip up north.

He drove us past the local hemp fields, and all the way to Bologna and then down through Florence. On the way back to Naples we decided to stop and visit San Marino, but by the time we got there—driving up an incredibly steep and narrow mountain road—everything was shut down. As Carl drove the car carefully back down the mountain, we began to pick up speed—far too much speed. The brakes had failed! Carl was livid since he had just had them fixed the previous day. He cursed at the poor workmanship and the lazy Italian workmen, all the while pumping the brakes and furiously downshifting. My mother grabbed onto my arm so hard that I had bruises for a week.

My mind was flooded with thoughts of all the car accidents involving the Ferraro men. All I could think of was, Here's yet another Ferraro male about to be engaged in a fatal car accident. I closed my eyes and prayed as Carl continued to downshift through the gears and pump the brakes. Somehow he managed to keep us on the road. When we reached bottom and were still alive, I felt like crying. I just wanted to go home.

I was angry with Carl, although my mother thought he was a hero for saving us. I grumbled that he should have made sure his car was working properly before driving it up a mountain.

My feelings about Carl were confused. I loved my brother very much. I had admired him from afar for a long time. But I couldn't understand why he wasn't more generous and open with my mother. He and I were of different minds about her. I felt protective. I was passionate about someday taking care of her, easing her burden, and insulating her from hardship. Carl seemed to feel none of that protective instinct, but of course he had never had the opportunity to spend time with her as I had. He had gone from military school to college to the army—and then to Italy. He didn't know what life was like for our mother, and he didn't ask. I thought he took advantage of her immense love for him.

I was also astute enough to realize that we had been raised for the most part separately, and that a significant loss had taken place in our lives at very different ages. I didn't doubt that there was sibling rivalry in our relationship. On some level we were both fighting to be the one who was loved the best—and perhaps, too, to be recognized as the one who was most shattered by the loss of our father.

John Zaccaro and I started dating seriously once he was discharged from the Marine Corps and started working in his father's business. My mother and I began to meet his extended family. Often on the weekends we'd be invited to Bay Shore to dine with the relatives. My mother got to eat lobster again, which she loved but had not had since my father died.

One Sunday we were enjoying a wonderful dinner with John's family at a waterfront restaurant that overlooked Long Island's Great South Bay. My mother looked beautiful that day. She was seated next to one of John's uncles—a big, effusive bear of a man. He was a nice man, but very loud, a nonstop talker who constantly illustrated his points with sweeping gestures of his hands.

I was sitting across the table from him and my mom, next to John. A couple of times I noticed my mother squirming a bit, trying to inch away. Just as the lobster was being served, John's uncle made a joking remark to my mother. As he did so, he put his arm around her and squeezed her close to him. My mother's face registered pure shock and horror. Today a gesture like that wouldn't mean anything, and I'm sure his intentions were purely familial. But my mother had been raised in a time when such an embrace came only from a husband. A casual squeeze from a stranger was something reserved for prostitutes and loose women. I could see the thought racing through my mother's mind. She was thinking John's uncle assumed that because she was without a husband, she was a loose woman. She could be toyed with. Her humiliation was palpable.

Before I even realized what I was doing, I had risen to my feet. My eyes were on fire—I was burning with outrage. I leaned across the table and yelled, "Get your hands off my mother!"

Everyone froze. John's uncle released his grip. My mother looked shocked. John looked pale. I sat back down. Everyone was staring at me. I started eating my lobster. So did everyone else. Eventually, regular conversation returned to the room. I can only imagine what they were thinking. I'm sure there was more than a little talking among the aunts, uncles, cousins, nieces, and nephews in the days to come.

But it didn't really matter what anyone thought. I felt extremely protective of my mother. Not that John's family wasn't always lovely to her, but there were so many of them and so few of us. What was most important to me under any circumstance was that she simply be treated with respect. My mother had earned it a thousand times over.

Clearly, John was only now starting to comprehend the full impact, the totality, of what he was in for. He loved me, and I him, but I'm not sure he was ready for the complete package. One day he said, "Gerry, I don't want you to work after we're married."

I didn't say anything. I just looked at him with obvious disbelief. He smiled. I smiled back.

"Really," he said.

"John, I'm a lawyer," I finally responded, surprised that this was even a conversation.

"My mother never worked," John replied, as if that were reason enough.

I had to remind myself how dramatically different our lives had been. We might as well have been raised oceans apart instead of miles. John's mother had never needed to work, hadn't been raised to work. John's paternal grandparents had been born in this country—he was a third-generation American. His family was successfully established, the immigrant experience a distant memory. The intrinsic scrappiness of the newcomer had been transformed into the more blasé expectation of the long-arrived. The Zaccaros no longer felt they had to prove themselves.

The other big difference was that the Zaccaro family was rigorously centered on the men. John's father, John's older brother, Frank, and John formed a dominant troika both at home and at work. The matriarch of the clan, Rose Zaccaro, was a very private woman—tough in her own way, but naturally deferential toward her husband.

It wasn't that I was a total feminist by any means. The truth is, at twenty-four my sense of myself as an adult woman was barely formed. Memories of my father were distant. I had been raised almost entirely in a world of women. The adults who had been my role models for authority and power were the nuns and my mother. Since there had been no strong men in my life to defer to, I had never learned to do so.

I had been trained and educated to make whatever I wished of myself, but I had never really considered how I would balance my professional aspirations with the personal demands of being a wife and mother. What John saw as a simple either-or didn't seem so simple to me.

Even though these thoughts initially troubled me, I was able to mask any trepidation I may have experienced. I wasn't going to let my training go to waste. Nor was I going to deny myself the chance for love and family. I was confident that there was a way to make good things happen if sincerity, intelligence, and devotion were applied. Besides, I stood on the precipice of a new world of opportunity for women, and I trusted that my conflicting dreams would eventually sort themselves out. That never seemed so clear to me as on the day I graduated from law school. As I stood with my classmates, my mother and fiancé cheered me on from the audience. I had reached yet another milestone, thanks to my mother's faith and persistence. I would put it to good use. Now it was time I started giving back.

Earlier, I had tried to put my thoughts on paper—to let my mother know exactly how grateful I was. Before the ceremony, I slipped a card into her purse. It read:

> Dearest Mommy,
>
> It's a waste of time to write you a thank you note because if I ever do it adequately it would take volumes and volumes and this little piece of paper could never do it. Nevertheless, I want you to know how much I appreciate everything you've done for me through the years and now I feel it's my turn to stop taking and start giving. God took Daddy. But He certainly knew what He was doing when He gave me a mother like you. You're everything I want to be and will try to be with time. Many, many thanks for everything.
>
> Love,
> Gerry
>
> P.S. Stop crying.

Two days before my wedding to John I had taken the New York State Bar exam, so my maiden name appeared on all my papers. When it came time for me to be admitted to the bar, I had the option of changing to my married name, Zaccaro. And certainly, in

1960, that was the obvious thing to do. Women just didn't keep their maiden names after marriage. But it wasn't that automatic with me. I thought about it long and hard, and finally approached John with my conclusion.

"Would you be upset if I wanted to practice law under the name Ferraro? If it weren't for my mother, I would never have gotten through law school. I'd like her to feel that the name will be used, that the degree belongs to her, too."

John shrugged. "Whatever you want," he said. He gave me his sleepy smile. I think he must have figured, Sure, what difference would it make? I wasn't going to be practicing law anyway. I was going to be raising a family.

And that's exactly what I did for the next thirteen years. Donna was born in 1961, John in 1964, and Laura in 1966. Before I had children, I worried that I wouldn't be able to bear the existence of a stay-at-home mom. My mind and heart were always churning. I needed action, discovery, growth, exploration. How would I ever transform myself into a patient, stable mother? I had few role models. My own mother had always worked, and most of the young mothers I knew didn't have the advantage of the education or the expectations that had always defined my life.

But I wasn't prepared for my first sight of Donna. The moment I glimpsed the sweet face of my first child, my heart melted. I immediately knew that the last thing I wanted was to let her out of my sight. Donna had dark curly hair and deep brown eyes, which she inherited from her father. Her spirit and spunk reminded me of myself as a child.

I've heard it said that while the firstborn in a family often receives the most attention, he or she must also suffer from the most trial and error. This was true for Donna. My mothering skills had not yet relaxed with experience; I was wound too tight. I filled every moment of Donna's young life with learning. At four years of age, she was taking tap dancing and swimming and learning to play the violin. In her spare time she was reading and doing math problems. I was really too much! I wanted my daughter to be perfect, and my greatest regret to this day is that I pushed her too hard. She was *already* perfect the day she was born.

I was easier on John Jr., who was born a little more than two years after Donna. And by the time Laura came along, two and a half years after that, I'd achieved some balance. I allowed Laura to be two years old at two, and three years old at three—just the way it was supposed to be.

I marveled at the unique delight each child brought, and how completely they won my heart. I was grateful for every day I had with them, and I saw for myself the truth that so many women have discovered—that you can't possibly know the depth of mother love until you have experienced it yourself. Now I could grasp my mother's heartbreak at the tragic death of Gerard. Remembering how guilty she had felt about crying for him, I told her how brave I thought she was. "If it were me, I don't think I would have ever stopped crying," I said, and I meant it.

My children allowed me to experience the full pleasure of family life. I basked in it, thankful for the chance to create the environment of togetherness I had been deprived of in my own childhood. I especially loved watching Donna and Laura together. I had never had a sister, and it was obviously something very special.

My mother was experiencing a similar joy. Her grandchildren became the center of her life. It was as if every moment she had missed with Carl and me was being returned through them. I shivered whenever I thought of her spending all those years apart from the only thing that gave meaning to her life—her children. When the kids were young, my mother often said to me, "Listen to your children. They are human beings—people—no matter how young they are. Treat them with respect, and they will give you respect."

She also said, "Give your children all the care they need, and more if possible, and give them every minute you can. Giving love gives happiness, and without happiness there is nothing."

John, too, was transformed by parenthood. Although his parents were wonderful people, it wasn't their way to demonstrate lavish displays of affection. As a boy, John had worshiped his father, but there was no playfulness in their relationship, few hugs and kisses. John once told me that during the summers growing up, he, his mother, and Frank stayed out at a beach house all week, while his father worked in the city. John would wait at the train station for his father's arrival on Friday nights with breathless excitement. "When I saw him, I would start to cry, I was so happy," he once told me. "But I didn't run into his arms."

Unlike his father, John was an effusive and adoring dad, who couldn't wait to finish work so he could be with the children. He would move heaven and earth for them, and I doubt that he ever missed a single event in their lives. At the end of the day, when John's car pulled up to our house, on Deepdene Road, he was instantly surrounded by three ecstatic children, fighting for hugs and kisses.

I often told my mother during those years that I wished only to be half the mother she was, because she was so exceptional. I knew, however, that the 1960s signaled a new era for women, and the kind of role model I would be for my daughters and my son would be different, unconventional. I was going to do something with what I'd learned. I just wasn't sure what form that would take—yet.

I took after my mother in one regard. Nothing was more important than my children's education. Education was the difference between controlling your life and having it controlled by others. For me, it represented the opportunity to move out of the slavish existence that had been my mother's. But it also meant something more. The value of education transcended the economic. It was the force that shaped a person's view of the world, philosophy of life, commitment to others, and moral resolve. I had seen the narrow-mindedness, bigotry, and rigidity that were produced by ignorance. My children would be taught to look beyond the confines of their own race, ethnicity, religion, and lifestyle.

Unfortunately, even in the best schools, these lessons sometimes had to be learned the hard way.

When John Jr. was six, he arrived home from school one day with a guilty look that I knew meant trouble. With some prodding, he said that I would be getting a call from the headmaster.

"What did you do?" I asked.

He looked down at the floor and mumbled, "I punched a guy."

"John, that's terrible!" I said with dismay. We had always enforced a very strict no-hitting policy. "Why did you do that?"

The story came out that an Irish kid in his class had called him a wop.

I asked John, "Do you know what that means?"

He shook his head. "No . . . but I could tell by the way he said it that it was something bad."

I told John that it was very wrong to hit someone, and it was also very wrong to call people ugly names. When the headmaster phoned to complain about John's behavior, I said, "I agree that it was very wrong for John to punch that child. However, I'm not going to punish him. And I hope your next phone call will be to the other child's parents to ask them why they are teaching him to use terms like wop in their home."

I knew it came from the parents. Kids have to be taught to hate.

Restlessness was a natural state for me. I've always had a tremendous reservoir of energy, an extra battery—and so I seemed to gravitate toward activism. I was an active parent, involved in the community and the schools, always looking for ways to improve situations.

During the summers, I spent wonderful weeks with the children on Fire Island, but even then I was looking for things to do. My efforts weren't always successful, nor were they always wise. I really knew I was out of line the year I inadvertently took on the Fair Harbor Volunteer Fire Department, which was as sacred a cow as you'd ever see.

One day I was sitting on the beach watching the kids and talking to my neighbors Gladys and Elsie. Gladys and her husband were both in their seventies. Elsie was my age, and she was single and staying with her parents. We were chatting about the volunteer fire department and how, during the week, there were only a few older men manning the station. Gladys's husband, who had recently had a heart attack, and Elsie's father, who was approaching eighty, were two of the mainstays.

I expressed my concern that if there were a serious fire during the week, when the island was populated mostly by women and children, these old guys might have some trouble handling it.

"I think the fire department should start accepting women," I said. "We could do the job."

It was as if I had dropped a bomb on the beach. The two women were horrified. Apparently, they told the men what I had said, and there was quite an upheaval about it. It was unthinkable that women could invade the sanctuary of their all-men club. I was nearly booed out of town. It sure didn't say very much for my early political instincts. And thank goodness there was never a fire at our house!

During the winters, I kept mentally busy by doing pro bono work for women in Family Court, and I became increasingly politically active. In 1968, I was elected, along with Isabel Shanley, to be the first woman to serve on the board of the Forest Hills Gardens Corporation. I became a community activist and joined a group fighting against a plan to build apartments using the air rights over the Long Island Rail Road. We were concerned about congestion, but we knew nothing about zoning. Finally, we raised the money and hired a young lawyer from Brooklyn who had just negotiated a public housing fight in Corona, Queens, and was being widely praised. His name was Mario Cuomo. He was brilliant. Cuomo won the case, and although it was later reversed in the Court of Appeals, we all became big Mario Cuomo fans.

In 1970, I was elected president of the Women's Bar Association at a time when we were battling to have a voice in the selection of judges. Not only were we not asked to review judicial candidates, as a committee of the regular Bar Association did, but we were concerned that women candidates who went before the established committee had trouble getting ranked "highly qualified." When Marie Lambert, a prominent woman lawyer who was then president of the New York Trial Lawyers Association, did not receive a "highly qualified" rating before the Bar's judicial committee, I set up a review process and brought her before a committee of the Women's Bar Association. The difference between our review and that of the other Bar Association's was that we didn't consider her gender a disqualifying factor. I also invited all of the other candidates and issued a press release with our findings. There was a bit of grumbling about whether we had standing, but the following year, all candidates showed up for the screening. After that, it was just a matter of course. I was learning fast that only if you exert authority do you receive it.

As my youngest daughter, Laura, entered the second grade, I began thinking about returning to work. I had agreed to stay home while the children were young, but once they were in school full-time I would pursue my career. I wanted to get a real job practicing law. In November of 1973, a perfect opportunity presented itself to me.

My cousin Nick Ferraro had been elected Queens district attorney, and I wanted to fill one of the hundred vacancies for assistant prosecutors in his office. There were only two problems—I had no experience in criminal law, and the fact Nick was my cousin had the appearance of nepotism. I took care of the first problem by studying the Criminal Code, which had changed in the thirteen years since I had graduated from law school. The second problem was overcome by the committee's scrutiny of me, headed by Mario Cuomo. If I got by the committee, I had the job. In January 1974, along with eighty-six other assistant DAs, I was sworn into office. My first government job.

John was completely supportive of my return to work. He knew that for me, as for him, family would always come first, and he wanted me to use my training. I explained to the children that it was important for me to use what I'd learned—what my mother and I had worked so hard for. They didn't have a problem with my decision, especially since my mother—their Nan—now lived only a few blocks away and would be spending more time with them. She had finally retired the previous year. My mother and my children had a very special relationship, and sometimes it wasn't such a bad thing if Mom got out of the way.

After thirteen years, it was the first time I went to work outside the home. I initially took some ribbing over my family ties to Nick, but I let it be known that the boss's cousin was a team player. I put the same intensity into my work as I put into my life. My efforts certainly let my colleagues know that I wasn't hired because of my connections to the boss. It didn't matter what had to be done to make a case work; I'd do it. It was the way I worked. I also got along well with the cops and my (mostly male) colleagues. I could discuss sports or police reports with equal animation and knowledge. John was a huge Rangers and Mets fan, and you pick up sports trivia and lore by osmosis when you're married to a zealot.

My closest relationship in the DA's office wasn't with another attorney but with a secretary named Pat Flynn. We came from similar backgrounds. Pat had children about my kids' ages, and she had also fairly recently returned to the world of work. Pat worked for three other attorneys besides me, but we often found time to have lunch together. We'd talk about our kids, our husbands, and mundane office stuff. We became friends. When I left the DA's office, I made sure Pat Flynn had a new job, too. And when I finally made it to Congress, Pat Flynn was the manager of my New York office. I eventually practiced my vice presidential nomination acceptance speech in front of her. She became one of my most trusted advisers.

The DA's office opened my eyes to a grim side of life. I handled arson cases, rape cases, and quickly became known for my ability to work with the children who were crime victims. My strong maternal feelings came through in those situations, as I had a natural empathy for their suffering. My time as an elementary-school teacher also came in handy. I was able to use innocuous questions and meandering conversations to weave a web of facts about a crime.

Experience after experience with children, women, the elderly—those who were victimized in the worst sense—gave shape to my political philosophy. I believed that the role of government was to protect and defend individuals as well as the nation. We were the greatest military and economic power in the world, but we hadn't found a way to make sure our children and our elderly were safe.

In September 1977, after my cousin Nick had left the DA's office, I was named to head a new unit, dealing with crimes against the elderly, child abuse, and domestic violence against women; it was called the Special Victims Bureau. It was a challenging and frustrating task that left me drained and angry. The most violent and horrible experiences became my daily reality. I felt helpless. Lives were destroyed by sick, violent criminals long before the cases ever found their way to my desk. I was often the last chance for any justice to be done. The harrowing nature of the cases took its toll on me. After listening to the grim tales of violence and sexual abuse, day after day, I developed an ulcer.

The most devastating case I handled—and the one that would haunt me forever after—was the rape of a six-year-old girl, named Lisette, by an eighteen-year-old neighborhood boy, named Caesar Bones. High on angel dust, Bones accosted Lisette on her way to the store and dragged her behind some bushes. There he raped and sodomized her so brutally that after vaginal surgery she required two weeks in the hospital.

I was determined to put Bones away—to make sure he never touched another child. But it nearly broke my heart to call the fragile, traumatized little Lisette to testify before a grand jury. Intellectually, it was easy to justify asking a child to testify. Without her testimony, Bones would walk—free to attack another little girl. But on a human level, as a mother, it was the worst part of my job. I wanted only that Lisette be able to forget this ever happened to her—yet I was asking her to remember.

Seated in the grand jury room, a pretty little girl with a sweet, trusting face, Lisette answered each of my questions. She was doing very well. Then I very gently asked her to tell us what happened when Caesar took her behind the bushes. All of a sudden, she started to scream, "I want my mommy!" Nearly in tears from the pain of the situation, I picked Lisette up and carried her outside to her mother. Lisette huddled in her mother's arms. She was inconsolable and wanted to go home. She didn't want to talk about it. As her mother tried to comfort her, I felt lousy. If this had been my child, I might have whisked her away. The instinct was so great to let her go. But as a prosecutor, I had to get Caesar Bones. Speaking quietly but forcefully, I urged Lisette's mother to convince her to testify.

Finally, Lisette agreed and we returned to the grand jury room. But almost as soon as I began asking questions, her face started to crumble. I lifted her up, sat down in the witness chair, and put her in my lap. I put my arms around her and cradled her. After advising the court reporter to simply record my words, not my actions, I very softly began asking her questions—as if she and I were alone in the room. Slowly she began to answer. I got the indictment.

It certainly made me even more cautious than I might normally have been with my own children. I made it a habit to carefully monitor their whereabouts at all times. They weren't allowed to walk anywhere alone after dark, even in their own neighborhood. I had to know where they were going, and they were almost always required to call as soon as they'd arrived at their destination, no matter what time it was.

In the midst of running the Special Victims Bureau, I inadvertently discovered that my salary was several thousand dollars less than the other Bureau chiefs—all of them men—were being paid. When I asked my boss about it, he looked genuinely surprised at my question and said, "But, Gerry, you have a husband."

"So what?" I responded. "They have wives." I was livid. And I was growing increasingly frustrated. There were too many barriers stacked up, preventing our really doing anything to help all of the people who needed help. The justice system was an endless, staggering, inexplicable bureaucracy with a thousand functionaries doing their thing—not necessarily with enthusiasm or competence. Meanwhile, the victims were continually revictimized by the very system that was supposed to prosecute their assailants. There weren't enough shelters for battered women. There were no recovery centers for elderly victims of violence. There weren't enough foster homes, and no adequate therapy, for the horribly abused children I'd seen. There was no legislation in the works to do anything about it, either.

One winter evening, I was driving from a bar mitzvah of one of the neighborhood kids with Mario Cuomo, who was now the lieutenant governor, and his wife, Matilda. I was describing the pain I witnessed every day, and my frustration at being helpless to stop it. "I'm thinking about quitting and running for public office," I said, finally giving voice to my private thoughts.

"What about Congress?" Mario said immediately. I looked at him and laughed. To be honest, I hadn't set my sights that high. But now I thought, Why not?

"What about Congress?" I asked him back. The very next day I began preparing for what, at age forty-two, would become one of my greatest passions and my life's work.

• SEVEN •

THE PEOPLE'S BUSINESS

My parents were always too busy earning a living to find the time for politics, but they were both extremely patriotic. As an immigrant to America, my father's proudest moment came on the day he was granted his U.S. citizenship. The day he cast his first vote as an American citizen was also a benchmark. He aligned himself with the more labor-friendly—meaning more immigrant-friendly—Democratic Party. Seeing the havoc wrought by the Great Depression, he was an avid believer in Franklin Delano Roosevelt's New Deal.

My mother arrived at her political philosophy from a different direction. Born in America to a poor and struggling immigrant family, she had not grown up experiencing the wonders of the American dream. Her street in East Harlem hadn't been paved with gold. Once she married and began to achieve some comfort in

Newburgh, she was eager to protect it. Seeing the GOP as more solicitous of those with business and property to maintain, she became a staunch Republican.

Although I was only a small child, I still retain a vague recollection of my parents' election day squabbles. They always took me with them as they headed to the polls. It seemed that their sole mission was to cancel out each other's vote. After my father's death, my mother became concerned about the new disparity. She felt guilty that his side was no longer being represented. It troubled her to the point that she finally became a Democrat. She needn't have worried. It would soon become clear that in me the Ferraros had produced the staunchest Democrat of all.

Unlike the Irish Americans, who had long dominated the leadership in the Democratic Party, Italian Americans could not be taken for granted as a voting bloc. They were proud to be Americans, but slow to trust the government or turn over their loyalty to a particular political machine. True loyalty was reserved for the family. Even the venerated Catholic Church did not merit unconditional surrender. Most of all, again because of where they came from, Italian Americans distrusted the bureaucracy of government. There was an inherent fear of dependency on the state—which is why my grandmother sent her young children to work rather than accept public assistance after my grandfather's stroke.

When Italian American candidates finally began to run for public office, even they didn't automatically garner support from their community. Fiorello La Guardia, the beloved mayor of New York City, wasn't elected on the strength of the Italian American vote. He won his mandate from liberal Jewish and black constituencies. Of course, La Guardia was hardly typical of the immigrant experience. He'd been raised as an Episcopalian in Arizona.

I wanted to win votes based on issues, not ethnicity. As I began my political career, I believed I could appeal to a cross section of voters. The things I cared about were precisely the same things most people cared about. If I had a concrete ideology, it was the democratic ideal—the ability to earn a living wage; being safe in one's neighborhood; quality education for all children; compassionate care and dignity for the elderly and disabled; strengthening the responsiveness and responsibility of the community. I wanted to make sure there was going to be something left to pass on to our children—a legacy of freedom, possibility, and security. I sought to make a tangible difference—the very difference I was unable to make in the DA's office.

I was passionate about justice, but I'd already learned that true justice doesn't happen in the criminal justice system, which could punish the wrongdoers but not prevent the crimes. There had to be a way to restructure our communities, change the atmosphere that permitted its most vulnerable citizens to suffer in the first place. I admit that I'd always been tough on crime, but the Special Victims Bureau reinforced my resolve a thousandfold. As a mother whose fundamental instinct was to protect her children, I was determined to make sure that more was done at a higher level to protect their futures from being destroyed by random acts of criminality. The only way to do that was to gain access to legislative power. And the only way to do that was to expose myself to the political process and run for office.

I began to explore the political landscape in my Queens district, and it didn't seem too promising. The Ninth Congressional District's incumbent congressman, James J. Delaney, was seventy-seven years old, had been in Congress for decades, and as Rules chairman wielded a lot of power. Everyone agreed that Delaney—a rock-hard conservative Democrat—couldn't be unseated. But when Republican assemblyman Al DelliBovi, a rabid conservative with the reputation of being a mean political street fighter, announced that he was running, Delaney unexpectedly decided to retire. The House seat that he'd warmed for more than thirty years came free. Patrick Deignan, a local Democratic leader, and Thomas Manton, a city councilman, immediately threw their hats in the ring. I announced a few weeks later, in May 1978, when I formed the Geraldine A. Ferraro for Congress Committee and filed with the Federal Election Commission.

One of the first things I had to take care of was the matter of my name. Would I run as Gerry Zaccaro, or Gerry Ferraro? We finally settled on Ferraro. The fact that my cousin Nick Ferraro already had name recognition as a successful local politician could send a few votes my way. My name, Gerry, might cause a problem because many people would naturally assume that Gerry was a man. So it was decided that from then on I would be known as Geraldine Ferraro.

The truth was that I'd gradually been paving the way for some kind of political run for a few years. I'd been a vigorous and loyal worker for the local Democratic Party. If there were dues to be paid, I'd paid them. And when I initially approached the local party leaders about running for Delaney's seat, everyone encouraged me . . . at least to my face. But once the preprimary machinery lurched into action, I found that I was being squeezed out. Donald Manes controlled the party, and he wanted a party regular. City Councilman Thomas Manton received the endorsement, with barely a nod in my direction. From what I could tell, my candidacy was going to be over before it started. I was unwilling to accept that. I flew to Washington and appealed directly to Delaney for his support. He apparently hadn't expected to have to actually deal with me. Nevertheless he was charming and courteous; but he blew me off like a pesky fly.

I was going to have to fight to get in. The Democratic Party wasn't pleased with me. I was viewed as a spoiler, a renegade—"someone on an ego trip" was how they put it. That's the last thing I'd wanted, but I'd been given little choice. I paid little attention to the negatives. If I waited to be asked to run, I never would be. What could I accomplish by being a wallflower, hoping the boys would ask me to dance? I had to go directly to the voters.

And of course, no one ever said it was going to be easy. It was a daunting prospect. I had to collect fifteen hundred signatures of registered Democrats to be eligible to appear on the primary ballot. At the same time, I had to try to reach out to all of the Democratic voters in the district. When I asked the local party organization to make the lists of registered Democrats available to me, I was ignored.

I was paralyzed momentarily, until my mother said, "Well, we'd better get started," and led a group of volunteers to the Board of Elections. For many days they sat at long tables, hand-copying the names of thousands of registered Democrats from the Ninth District, in Queens. My mother's hand was swollen but she was beaming when the task was completed. Overnight, she had turned into the wisest and most enthusiastic campaigner I'd ever seen. She thought this was a great way to spend her retirement.

My daughter Donna was sixteen and entering her senior year in high school. She enthusiastically volunteered to work with me on the campaign. John Jr. and Laura were eager to help out, but I wanted them to have some fun, so they spent most of their summer at camp. I missed them, but it turned out to be an incredible education for Donna and me.

Every morning by 6 A.M. we were standing outside a different subway station in Queens, passing out literature and collecting signatures. It was a tough sell. The district was 84 percent white and composed primarily of people who were of Irish, Italian, and Eastern European descent. A large percentage were blue-collar workers. This was Archie Bunker territory—in fact, the lead-in for the television show *All in the Family* had been filmed in my district. Donna and I were not always welcomed with open arms by the grumpy early-bird commuters. Many of them were blunt about how distasteful it was to see a wife and mother hawking herself in a public place. I wasn't offended. "Just sign the petition," I begged them. "You don't have to vote for me. It just gets me on the ballot." Even on the sultriest of summer days, with the temperature inching toward a hundred degrees, Donna and I would be out with a staffer getting signatures. We were both surprised to find that we were actually having fun. It was a new aspect of our relationship—a portent of the future. Donna was still my baby, and she always would be. But to be with her like this, to share the experience, to have her as an ally and a colleague—that was fantastic!

I had needed fifteen hundred signatures. By the deadline for filing, we had collected seven thousand—more than enough to make any challenge fruitless. I was on the primary ballot.

The next hurdle was money. Women candidates consistently are unable to call on the seemingly limitless resources of their male counterparts to raise funds. I was the absolute embodiment of that truism. Without party support, I was on my own. John's mother contributed $1,000, and some of the neighbors put in a few hundred. But the real money came from John and the kids. I was quite upset the day my three children announced that they were loaning me money from their college accounts. It didn't seem right, but they insisted. They wanted to help send Mom to Congress. I teased them: "Do you want me out of the house *that* badly?" With a generous contribution from their dad, I had enough money to compete. I felt like the luckiest and most loved woman in the world to have a family that believed in me so much.

It took a while, but eventually we discovered that no good intention goes unpunished. There was a problem. The contributions weren't legal. On the eve of the primary, I learned that the family loans were prohibited under rules of the Federal Election Commission. I was terribly shaken by this news, especially since an attorney I'd consulted—a former lawyer for the FEC—had assured me the loans were legal. He was wrong. Under the law, which had been changed the previous year to limit spousal contributions, no one except the candidate was allowed to contribute more than $1,000. I had to pull out all the stops and find a way to pay back my family, which I did. But this error—in my first run for office—would haunt me for many years to come.

I'd learned a lot as a prosecutor, and I learned even more as I campaigned all over Queens. It quickly became clear to me that the issues that concerned me touched a nerve in others as well. I visited dozens of senior citizen homes. I discussed social programs, Social Security, medical care, and anything else of concern to the elderly. Sometimes I brought my mother with me. She was my secret weapon. Safety, security, and crime had increasingly become hot button issues for the elderly, and for everyone else, too. In late July I delivered a sensible, comprehensive, and necessarily ambitious plan designed to reduce a spate of subway crime that had erupted in Queens in the last few years. Actually, the proposal could have been implemented a lot farther than just Queens. First, I made the eternal call for more subway cops, and I also urged the installation of security cameras, so that the platforms and other major areas of stations could be constantly monitored. I suggested a special transit court, set up just to handle the repeat subway crime offenders. From my days as a prosecutor I carried forward this significant statistic: in a city of over 8 million people, there were only four hundred or so persistent offenders, who committed more than *50 percent* of all the subway crime!

My outrage, my passion, my absolute conviction that I could make a significant difference finally had an effect. On primary day, I beat the other two candidates and won with a clear majority. Now all I had to do was win the general election. Both of my primary opponents endorsed me, but Congressman Delaney was another story. He decided to remain neutral. There was speculation that it stemmed from some long-standing feud between the Irish and the Italians in the Queens party, but I couldn't get him to budge, even when I flew down to Washington. On the other hand, the two Republican leaders in the state, Senator Jacob Javits and Attorney General Louis Lefkowitz, declined to endorse DelliBovi. They had seen his behavior and wanted no part of his dirty tactics.

It was a nasty campaign. Al DelliBovi went after me on anything he could think of—including religion.

Every Sunday I attended Mass with my family, then went on to campaign in front of several other churches. I was a pro-choice Catholic, and DelliBovi targeted this issue as my weakness. Every Sunday, a group of antiabortionists would follow me from service to service, forming a chorus of hecklers, loudly accusing me of endorsing murder. I tried to ignore them, although it's very hard to close your ears to chants of "Baby killer!" On one Sunday, I'd finally had enough. Approaching a particularly loud and vitriolic demonstrator, I got right up in his face and challenged him.

"Excuse me!" I addressed him. "Did I hear you just call me a murderer, a baby killer? I've spent the past four and a half years prosecuting baby killers. Just because people don't share your religious views doesn't mean that they're wrong and you're right."

I walked away, leaving a demonstrator, for once, wordless. I felt better after that. Disagree with me, fine. But don't call me a baby killer.

Meanwhile, my mother was on the phone day after day, working the voters. Her pitch was simple but effective. "This is Antonetta Ferraro," she would say. "I'm calling for my daughter, Geraldine. Will you vote for her?" Who could resist?

DelliBovi and I crisscrossed the district, going from candidate night to candidate night. These were wonderful opportunities to address the issues, to let the constituency see how very different our positions were. But I should have suspected that DelliBovi wouldn't be content to debate on the issues alone. Though he had agreed that there would be no personal attacks, it didn't take long for him to get personal. Just before one event, he decided to attack the choices we had made about our children's education, and paint me as an elitist who couldn't relate to the concerns of "the common people." He distributed flyers showing the private school that John Jr. attended. The flyer asked how I could know about public schools if I was sending my child to a private school. Of course, the flyer didn't mention that I had been a public school teacher for five years, while DelliBovi had taught in a parochial school before running for the assembly. My opponent assumed that the attack would leave me defenseless. What he didn't know was that I would be delighted to debate him on the subject of education any day of the week.

And I saw an opportunity. At one event, before a packed house at William Cullen Bryant High School, on Thirty-first Avenue in Queens, I pulled a flyer that had just been distributed out of my pocket and asked the audience to do the same.

"It's true," I admitted. "My son does go to a private school. It's called Choate. My husband and I have worked hard. We've done well in order to provide the best for our children. Is there something wrong with wanting my son to have the best education we can provide? Isn't that what we all want for our children?"

I saw people in the audience nodding. My mother, sitting in the front row, smiled. I leaned forward on the podium and spoke from my heart. "I'm a mother. What mother here tonight doesn't want the very best for your child? What father? Raise your hands. Anybody? No. I didn't think so. Of course not. We all want the best for our children." And then I added, "John F. Kennedy went to Choate. If my son turns out to be half the man he was, I will be a very proud mother."

DelliBovi raised the issue one more time at a subsequent candidates' event, and I responded in exactly the same way. I could see that the audience was on my side, and I guess he could see it too, because he never brought it up again.

That helped a lot, but I needed all the star power I could muster. I was battling for a congressional seat in a very conservative district. President Carter even sent his very popular mother, Miss Lillian, to coax some votes out for me, and she brought a lot of media coverage with her. That seemed to throw DelliBovi and his supporters into an even greater frenzy. We weren't sure who did it, but windows were broken in my campaign office; picketers appeared outside of fund-raisers, accusing my husband and me of being slumlords; there were even rumors started that I was a lesbian.

The final blow came a week before the election, when DelliBovi exposed the campaign contributions that had been made by my husband and children but had been repaid. The Conservative Party of New York had already sent a stinging letter of rebuke to the Federal Election Commission, condemning "Ferraro's illicit campaign financing." My opponent was desperate.

And then the *New York Times* and the *New York Daily News* both endorsed me instead of DelliBovi. The *News* reminded its readership that DelliBovi had once made its list of ten worst legislators. The *New York Times* called me a "shrewd campaigner."

On a cold November election day in 1978, I stood at a blackboard in my campaign headquarters and jotted down the figures as they came in. At one point, the *Congressional Quarterly* called the election for DelliBovi, but the verdict was premature. It looked like I appealed to enough law-and-order conservatives after all. I won the election with 54 percent of the vote. I was going to Washington as the Democratic congresswoman from the Ninth Congressional District, in Queens, New York.

I was determined to do it all. Be a totally committed congresswoman in Washington and a fully engaged wife and mother in Queens, work for the good of the nation while also caring for the smallest needs of my local district. I promised myself that I could do it, or I wouldn't have taken the job. Others had done it, and so would I.

The new title of Congresswoman didn't replace the old title of Mother. I had no intention of becoming merely a voice over the long-distance wires. I settled on a schedule that would keep my life in some balance. I'd be in New York from Thursday night until Tuesday morning every week. Then I'd catch the shuttle to Washington early Tuesday morning. Thursday night I'd return home to my district. The two nights a week I spent in Washington, I worked late and fell into bed. My small apartment's refrigerator was usually empty.

None of this would have been possible without John's support. The man who had announced before our marriage that he didn't want his wife to work was now my greatest supporter. When I reflected on this change, I realized that John had always respected women, and regarded them as equals—it was part of what attracted me to him in the first place. Over the years that I'd spent in the DA's office, John had come to see that I could make a contribution to the world and still put my family first. He never felt threatened by anything I did. He was the most secure man I'd ever known.

When I arrived in Congress in 1979, there were only seventeen women in the House and Senate. By 1983, the number had inched up to twenty-four. The Hill had long ago shaped itself as the ultimate men's club, and its members—if they bothered at all—paid the barest lip service to issues concerning women.

What were those issues? They had never really changed very much, though those threatened by the thought of women having an equal voice in affecting the governance of the nation often referred to a "feminist agenda," as if women were secretly plotting the destruction of mankind. The real women's issues were bound up in economics. Women had been getting the short end of the stick on every count for generation after generation. The fastest-growing class of poor in our society was women and children. In my Queens district alone, there were 25,667 households officially headed by women. Without regard to their work, most of them were paid far less than their male colleagues. The typical woman was being paid a little more than half of what men in similar positions earned.

My eyes were also opened to the very real struggles that older women faced when it came to collecting benefits, especially pensions. Countless elderly women came to my office in Queens, desperate and without a source of income after their husbands died. It was shocking to realize that 2.8 million women over the age of sixty-five lived in poverty—in America.

Many of the issues that mattered to me first took root in the lives of my mother and my grandmother, and by extension the other women in my family. Equal rights, pensions, widows' benefits, health care, contraception, abortion all needed to be directly addressed, and legislated if possible. My life shone before me as a firsthand example of how potent it was to be treated equally—I had always been encouraged to be equal—and conversely it reflected the price my mother and grandmother were forced to pay when they were prohibited from enjoying the very freedoms I took for granted. It wasn't that there were laws *against* women being treated equally. It was a cultural prohibition that had existed for generations and generations—an accepted gender bias.

I used my time in Congress well, and in 1981 I introduced a bill to make private pensions fairer, and to recognize marriage as an economic partnership. It didn't even make it out of the gate. My female colleagues and I were introducing other bills on day care, alimony, child support, nondiscrimination in insurance, maternity leave, and tax credits for hiring displaced homemakers. For the most part, these bills languished in committees. The gender gap, as it was now being termed, was as wide on the Hill as it was in the nation. To have a voice, we needed power, and we found that power in a uniquely female way—through collaboration. We packaged our separate bills into one and introduced the Women's Economic Equity Act in 1983. By joining together, we were able to force an open debate on the issues. Some of the legislation passed—including my pension equity proposal.

What we did in Washington had the power to change lives. The policy we made translated into tangible results on the grassroots level. But we were fighting an uphill battle against a wave of antigovernment sentiment that swept Ronald Reagan into office in the 1980 presidential election. The Reagan administration wasted no time in uttering pious sentiments while setting about dismantling the fragile structure of protections we had built around the poor, the elderly, and the children of this country. The defining moment of my political life was Reagan's budget proposal, delivered shortly after his election in 1980: a $750 billion tax cut over five years, with an increase in defense spending. It was clear where the tax cut would be coming from—the very programs designed to protect the nation's poorest. It was a cynical proposal—and deadly.

Ronald Reagan's policies gave new clarity to my political philosophy. Who were we as a people? What had my mother and grandmother worked for? What legacy would my children and grandchildren inherit? What were the values that we held sacred? How could a nation be considered great when its children were deprived of nutritious lunches? How could a nation be considered great when its elderly were cast aside with no resources? How could a nation be considered great when it chose to build vast war machines, using the country's resources without regard to cost? Were we boosting an economy on the backs of the working poor? Down on the street, where it mattered, these choices translated into matters of life and death. I fought Reagan's budget proposals, and I knew I was right. Even my conservative Queens district continued to reelect me with wide margins.

As we approached 1984, the gender gap was widening. The disparity between male and female voters was growing. The issues women cared about the most had been relegated to a back burner, where they were simmering away. It was time to turn up the heat.

• EIGHT •

THE DAUGHTER OF AN IMMIGRANT

A few days after I was nominated as Walter Mondale's vice presidential running mate, in 1984, Gloria Steinem said that a jogger, a black man in his thirties, ran past her and recognized her. As he glided by he smiled and said, "Isn't it great? Now *you* can be president."

And she yelled back, "No, *you* can be president."

The black man grinned and said, "Now *any of us* can be president."

There was a real swell of excitement, the sense of new possibility and pride that surrounded my nomination. I had no idea how deeply the country would react to it.

It was an extraordinary event, and it took me a while to register the momentousness of the occasion. No woman had ever been so close to the most powerful office on earth—"an election away from a heartbeat away," as *Time* put it. No woman had ever before received such a vote of national confidence. Sixty-four years after female suffrage, I was being called "a living symbol of change." As he accepted the presidential nomination, Walter Mondale stated: "When we speak of the future, we speak of Gerry Ferraro." Because of my nomination, Democrats in thirty-two states formed teams to bring out unregistered women voters. The Women's Vote Project, a coalition of sixty-eight women's organizations in twenty states, worked in churches, Kmarts, and shopping centers, registering low-income women. The National Coalition of Black Voter Participation, the League of National Women Voters Education Fund, and the National Puerto Rico/Hispanic Participation Project all worked for this goal.

The initial moments of being a "first" is the headiest thing in the world. I can't begin to describe the overwhelming mix of thrill and terror I experienced. But when the last balloon has popped and the last roar has sounded from the crowd, you're left with exactly what you had before. You may be magnified in a million eyes, but you're still, after all, just you—with your convictions, your style, your life on display. I was an experienced politician, a fighter. But even I was completely unprepared for a national race. I knew what to do in a thunderstorm; a hurricane was an entirely different matter.

Truth be told, I'd never given myself much of a chance of being picked as Walter Mondale's running mate. Gary Hart seemed to have the best chance once his presidential bid was defeated, but there was also Senator Lloyd Bentsen, of powerful Texas. And there was another strong woman candidate, Dianne Feinstein, then the mayor of San Francisco. I was proud to see my name on the list of possibles, but I wasn't at all sure that the talk of a first woman vice presidential candidate was serious. Besides, I had other things on my mind. I had been appointed chair of the Platform Committee for the Democratic convention, and it was totally engaging work.

But the rumors wouldn't stop. After I traveled to North Oaks, Minnesota, to brief Mondale on the platform, the *New York Daily News* blared a speculative front-page headline with Mondale and me labeled RUNNING MATES? Immediately after that meeting, Mondale called me "one of the rising stars" of our party. I was flattered. The next day, Lane Kirkland, head of the powerful AFL-CIO, told Mondale that choosing a woman as his running mate would help his candidacy. NOW—the National Organization for Women—also backed me. There seemed to be a rising tide of opinion that out of the incredible mix of vice presidential possibilities Mondale was considering—Henry Cisneros, Tom Bradley, Wilson Goode, Lloyd Bentsen, Dianne Feinstein, Hart, me—he was planning to move in a radically different direction. I still thought the nomination would go to a man—unless by the time I was interviewed Mondale was running at least fifteen points behind in the polls.

Two weeks before the convention I traveled to Minnesota again, this time for my interview as a potential vice presidential running mate. Mondale was fifteen points behind in the polls. The largest union in the AFL-CIO, the United Food and Commercial Workers Union—1.3 million members, half of whom were women—endorsed me for the vice presidency as I flew out there the morning of the interview.

The interview went well enough, but in the days immediately following there were a number of negative leaks to major newspapers that described the interview as "not up to expectations" and "somewhat disappointing." Other articles speculated that I was "a little too flashy, a little too flip." Not only that, but the women interviewed—Martha Layne of Kentucky, Feinstein, and me—were compared to one another, rather than to any of the men who'd been interviewed, which really got my dander up. A continuous barrage of negative leaks emerged from the Mondale staff, so that I decided to fire back. It was one thing to be considered for a position. It was another to be pilloried for it! I didn't care about some hypothetical vice presidency. I cared about my six years of hard work in Congress and my eventual hopes for a run at the Senate. I cared about my reputation.

I called two friends of mine from Congress, Barbara Mikulski and Tony Coelho, and complained at great length. I asked Barbara to deliver a message directly to Walter Mondale. "Tell him, if he doesn't want me as his running mate, fine. But don't put me down as not being smart enough or capable enough to do the job. There's no need to destroy me in order to give him an excuse to turn me down."

The campaign of leaks and innuendo continued unabated. It just served to remind me anew that it was always tougher for a woman. It wouldn't have been politically expedient to just throw up my hands and say to hell with it. It would have served too many other people's aims, and it would have signaled a lack of grace under fire. It makes it too easy for political opponents looking for your vulnerabilities. There are always plenty, if you want to play that game. But I didn't want to waste my time doing that. If the attacks had come from the Republicans, at least I could understand it, but these were coming from high up in Mondale's staff.

On July 8, two days before I was to head out to San Francisco for the convention, a big story in the *New York Times* claimed that my candidacy was comparable to "a roller coaster spin," in which I had "zoomed in popularity," only to see my aspirations "plummet after sessions with Mr. Mondale." I was burning. Right after reading this, my phone rang. It was Mondale. He assured me that he'd had nothing to do with the spate of leaks surrounding me. I asked him if he'd seen the day's *New York Times.* He hadn't. He promised to read it and call me back. And a half hour later, he did. Again he apologized, and promised that no more of this behavior on the part of his staff would be tolerated. I believed him, but I was seething with anger at the pounding I'd been subjected to. As a matter of fact, I'd reached the end of this particular piece of rope.

"I think you should take my name out of consideration, Fritz. I don't want to be a part of this process anymore."

But Mondale refused. "No. I'm seriously considering you as my running mate. And you have my word—there'll be no more negative stories about you."

As I arrived in San Francisco on July 10, I didn't know that Barbara Mikulski had just presented Mondale with the latest delegate survey from the National Women's Political Caucus—which favored nominating a woman for the vice presidency and placed me at the top of its list of possible choices.

In the space of less than a day, I was intensively grilled by two of Mondale's closest aides—Michael Berman, in New York, and John Reilly, who was already in San Francisco. Early the next morning, I called my husband at his office in New York from my suite at the Hyatt Embarcadero. I told him things looked pretty serious. "We have to decide," I said. "This might really happen. Do we really want to go through this? Is it the right thing for our kids?"

If John had protested or argued that national exposure would hurt our family, I probably would have given up the idea. Our stance had always been "family first." But John didn't say that. He had a deep respect for me and for my potential. He wanted to see me reach the highest peak.

"We'll deal with it" was John's quiet response.

"Is there anything we have to worry about?" I asked. As much as you love someone, there's no way of completely knowing everything they've done.

"There's nothing as far as I know," John said. That was good enough for me.

"Who do you love the best?" I teased him, bantering with a familiar phrase of ours.

"You," he automatically responded. I smiled and hung up the phone.

The rest of the day was a blur of phone calls and activity as I prepared a speech to be given that evening to a session of the World Affairs Council. Between calls, I worked on it with my aides Jan Kalicki and David Koshgarian. David, who was the legislative director of my Washington office, was doing double duty as a speechwriter. The speech would be on foreign affairs, one of my presumed weaknesses. I really dug in. I was also expecting a call from Mondale later that afternoon with the final word on his choice.

At four-thirty that afternoon, Mondale called. No matter what he said, I was determined to let him know that he would have my complete support. He asked me to be his running mate. My heart was pounding but my voice was steady. I told him that I would be honored. After I hung up the phone, I didn't move for several minutes. My head was full of thoughts of my father. I ached with the knowledge that he was not alive to witness this moment. He would have burst with joy and pride. If ever there was a fulfillment of his much cherished American dream, this was it. Not only was I the first woman chosen for this role, I was the first Italian American. I remembered my grandmother's shy, deferential way, her efforts to be invisible, as if she sensed her life was of no account in this great land. My own mother had bent tradition and worked out of her home, but she took no delight in her own achievements. It was me she looked to for hope.

How far we'd come in such a relatively short time; how much had been endured and accepted. Walter Mondale was courageous for choosing me. It was through such courage that change happened. I thought of John and the children—I'd call them first, and then my mother. I felt a surge of determination. I intended to do the very best I could, to make everyone's confidence well founded.

When I finally spoke to my mother, she gasped at the news. Her voice was the equivalent of a warm embrace as she murmured, "Oh, my Gerry. My girl. Your father is rejoicing in heaven."

Hesitantly, I shared my fear. "Can I do it? I hope I can do it."

The village of Terranova, buried in the hills of southern Italy, has changed little since my grandmother Maria Giuseppa Caputo left its gates more than a hundred years ago.

My grandmother's first home in America, 250 Mott Street, on the Lower East Side of New York, as it appeared in 1940.

My uncle Angelo Caputo started out selling ice from a pushcart while going to school at night. He eventually became quite prosperous.

The child in this picture is my mother, Antonetta Corrieri, around age six. The woman is my grandmother Maria Giuseppa Corrieri.

At fourteen, my mother *(left)* had a flair for fashion. Here she is with her niece Millie, her half sister Sarah's child, on the day of Millie's confirmation.

My paternal grandfather, Don Carlo Ferraro.

My paternal grandmother, Maria Alessandra Ferraro.

My father, Dominick Ferraro.

My father's sister, Amalia, and brother Carl were sent to live with a relative in America when they were children. Amalia, who died at age twenty-six, was thought to be a saint.

My parents on their wedding day, October 2, 1927, at Saint Lucy's Church in New York City.

My father with his first American car.

Carl and little Gerard.

Me at eighteen months in our apartment on Mill Sreet.

My father's brother Angelo. I later found out he was a hero in the Italian Resistance during World War II.

A recent picture of my childhood home on DuBois Sreet in Newburgh.

Mount Saint Mary's was a magnificent school, but
I was lonely as a boarder there.

Carl, my mother, and me. My mother always did my hair in ringlets.

Carl in Naples, 1953.

My grandmother Maria Giuseppa at age eighty.

My grandmother, raising a toast at a family wedding the year before she died.

My mother and me aboard the SS *Constitution* in 1957, heading for Italy. It was her first vacation since my father died.

My mother and I in Naples, 1957.

This is me with my second-graders at P.S. 57 in Queens.

Our 1978 Christmas photograph includes John's mother, Rose Zaccaro, and my mother, Antonetta. I had just been elected to Congress.

Campaigning as a family in 1984.

This picture of my mother and me shows how close we were, and how frail she had become. Her hands are gnarled from a lifetime of beading.

My mother didn't attend the 1984 Democratic convention because she was afraid to fly. But I took her for a tour of my campaign plane, and she was thrilled.

The Ferraro plot in Marcianise, Italy, where my grandparents and two of their children are buried. Notice the photographs inlaid on the stones.

Me, my mother, and Laura at our house in Queens.

A lemon tree still blooms in the courtyard of my father's childhood home in Marcianise.

On my visit to Italy in 1996. To my left are my cousin Maria and her husband, Angelo, with their daughter Maria. On my right are my cousin Carlo and his wife, Giovanna, with Maria's second daughter, Sonja.

The town of Marcianise today.

My daughters, Donna and Laura, and my granddaughter, Natalie.

"Oh, Gerry," she laughed, "who would make a better vice president than you?"

Within a few hours, I was secretly whisked out of San Francisco and jetted to North Oaks for the official announcement with Mondale, which was to take place the next day. On the other coast, John and our daughter Laura were being hustled and jostled with a fair amount of discretion so they could be brought out to be at my side. It turned out that Donna couldn't just pick up and leave—she had work. John Jr. was out of reach in Hawaii working on a cruise ship. So John and Laura flew out to Minnesota.

The next day, at Minnesota's state capitol, I stood beside Walter Mondale as he announced his decision. He had chosen me to run for vice president of the United States of America.

"This is an exciting choice," he said. I thought so.

Mondale was making history, and he had chosen me to make history with him. I was going to give it everything I had.

Two hours before I was scheduled to walk onto the biggest stage of my life, I called my mother, in Queens. I wanted to hear her voice, to pull her closer to me through the long-distance wires. She was not at the convention because her unshakeable refusal to fly precluded a trip across the country.

"I wish you were with me," I said.

"I *am* with you," she assured me. I could hear the bustle of activity and laughing voices on her end. My mother would not be alone. Her apartment was jammed. Carl, his wife, Teresa, and my nephews had decided to stay with her. John's mother was there, as were my aunts, my entire district office, and an NBC-TV film crew.

I could not have imagined the sensation of walking into the convention hall that night. With a force that could only be described as cosmic, I was carried on a wave of jubilation. The roar was deafening, and when I reached the platform and looked out into the hall, my first impression was: *This night belongs to women.* There were thousands of them, cheering, crying, waving. I'd heard that many male delegates had given their floor passes to women alternates, knowing it was a historic night for them.

When I finally spoke, I conceded my inability to express the depth of my feelings. "As I stand before the American people and think of the great honor this convention has bestowed upon me, I recall the words of Dr. Martin Luther King Jr., who made America stronger by making America more free. He said: 'Occasionally in life there are moments which cannot be completely explained by words. Their meaning can only be articulated by the inaudible language of the heart.' Tonight is such a moment for me. My heart is filled with pride."

I spoke to the crowds on the convention floor, the millions watching on television around the world, as if I were addressing my own family. In simple words I shared with them the magnitude of this moment. America, I said, had always stood for promise—not just for a privileged few, but for every citizen. That the daughter of an immigrant was standing on that stage was proof that the promise was real.

On this world stage, I wanted most of all to honor my mother, and to hold out a hand of hope to the next generation. "Tonight, the daughter of a woman whose highest goal was a future for her children talks to our nation's oldest party about a future for us all," I said. I looked down to where John and my children were seated. I had told the children not to cry, but they were fighting to hold back the tears. As I spoke my final words, the floodgates opened. I watched them sob as I said, "To my daughters, Donna and Laura, and my son, John Jr., I say: My mother did not break faith with me, and I will not break faith with you. To all the children of America, I say: The generation before ours kept faith with us, and like them, we will pass on to you a stronger, more just America."

As soon as I finished, my children bolted onto the stage and ran to me, crying, "Oh, Mom, oh, Mom." John embraced me, and we stood waving to the crowds, blinded by the lights.

Life was forever changed. Secret Service protection, security concerns, staff, scheduling, time constraints, necessary duties—all becomes a whirlwind of action and reaction. Less than two weeks after the convention, the Republicans launched their first attack on my candidacy. In the financial disclosure statements that I'd been filing in Congress for six years, I had taken the statutory exemption not to include information about my husband's finances. I wasn't the only member of Congress to do so—seventeen of my colleagues had done the same thing in 1983, with a greater number than that failing to indicate whether they were taking the exemption or not. In fact, the spousal exemption had been claimed a total of 101 times between 1979 and 1983. Interestingly, until my nomination to the vice presidency, no member had ever been challenged—or questioned—about taking the exemption. (And none has since, although a flurry of amended reports were filed almost immediately after mine was questioned.)

But that wasn't all. Not only were my ethics under attack for my having taken the statutory exemption; John's handling of a court-appointed conservatorship suddenly came into question, and several of his real estate dealings were being scrutinized. I was waiting for the 1978 campaign loans the Federal Election Commission questioned to be brought up—it was already general knowledge. This seemed like good strategizing on the part of the Republicans. Rather than let the campaign get off the ground and focus on Reagan's ongoing efforts to dismantle America's social programs, they wanted to keep us down with withering fire focused on our finances and ethics. I had thirty days after the announcement of my candidacy—until August 20—to file a financial disclosure report with Congress.

Under constant pressure from the press, my staff handed me a press release concerning my finances. I read it quickly—too quickly—and missed the clause that stated I would release my income tax returns on August 20 *and* that my husband would release *his* as well.

When John saw the release, he frowned and shook his head. "I told you I'd release a financial statement, not my tax returns."

"Don't worry about it, " I consoled him. "I'll take care of it. It was a mistake."

I really had no immediate idea how I was going to handle it. But I felt this was a problem I'd created, however inadvertently, and I'd have to find a way to correct it

I corrected it, all right. On August 12, as I was about to leave on a swing through California on my first solo campaign trip, I answered a reporter's question about my husband's finances at an airport press conference with my usual directness.

"I requested my husband to do that and he feels quite frankly that his business interests would be affected by releasing his tax returns. John told me: 'Gerry, I'm not going to tell you how to run the country, don't tell me how to run my business.' "

What had I just said? Wrong message. But I wasn't done yet. In an attempt to dismiss the subject with a lighthearted quip, I blurted out, "You people who are married to Italian men, you know what it's like."

Deliver me from myself. My tongue was leaping ahead of my mind. I meant, of course, that Italian men tend to be very private about their affairs. But it was interpreted by many as an ethnic slur. An ethnic slur? That was preposterous. I wished I could take back those words. But they were already out, flashing along the news wires.

The next week of campaigning was a nightmare. Every question came back to finances. FERRARO'S HUBBY WON'T BARE TAXES was the headline in the *New York Daily News.* I knew being the first woman candidate would be difficult. As the first Italian American on a national ticket, I had expected to endure stereotypical whisperings of ties to organized crime. As the partner in a two-career couple, I knew that our personal affairs would be closely examined. We'd been through this before and survived. But I underestimated the power of the storm. This was no longer the Ninth Congressional District in Queens, New York. This was a national contest, and the winds of rhetoric could rip your skin off.

There was a clear double standard at work, a search for any kind of faux pas. The day before I'd made my remark about Italian men, President Reagan, warming up for his weekly Saturday radio broadcast, had jocularly stated—over a live microphone—"My fellow Americans, I am pleased to tell you I just signed legislation which outlaws Russia forever. The bombing begins in five minutes." It was obviously a joke, but a dangerous, outrageous joke coming from the president of the United States. Yet Reagan's frightening joke received less media attention than my remark about Italian men.

The continuing conjecture about my husband's business affairs, the furor over financial disclosure, the congressional exemption all were used as a bludgeon to keep the focus off campaign issues and on the campaigner's— my—ethics. This would not have happened if I were a man; nor would it have been an issue if I were not Italian American. My opponents delighted in fanning the flames of old fears about "the mob," and the press ran with it because it made for more intriguing headlines than the issues I was talking about.

Finally, the 1978 campaign loans were thrown into the mix. Right-wing conservative Rupert Murdoch's *New York Post* had banner headlines proclaiming: GERRY'S HUBBY IN NEW STORM: CHARGE ZACCARO LIED ON CAMPAIGN FUNDS.

I knew the campaign would be tough. Now I knew it would also be dirty. David Stein, the former FEC lawyer who'd led us into this loan problem originally, had turned on us and was now claiming—first in the conservative newspaper *Human Events,* then to the national press—that his advice to us in the spring of 1978 had been the opposite of what it had been. He was supposedly an expert in election law, and it was on his advice that I'd borrowed the $134,000 from my family. This had blown up in my face just before the 1978 election, but I'd replaced the loans with my own money, paid a $750 fine in 1979, and it had been cleared up based on our undisputed representation that we'd acted out of reliance on Stein's mistaken legal advice. The Washington Legal Foundation lodged a complaint against me with the Committee on Standards of Official Conduct in Congress and with the Justice Department. Two other complaints, one from the Fund for a Conservative Majority and the other from John Banzhaf, a gadfly professor at the National Law Center of George Washington University, also were lodged against me. None of them were resolved until after the election, but all of them were eventually settled in my favor.

This put a ridiculous amount of pressure on Mondale, and he was forced to deal with it. He supported John's right not to release his tax returns, but it would have been a lot easier if it hadn't been an issue. Did I want John to release them? Sure. Would I ask him to? No. And Fritz Mondale—perfect gentleman that he was—never pressured John or me to reverse that decision.

In the midst of all this brouhaha, U.S. Attorney Rudy Giuliani, a Reagan appointee, suddenly called John to his office. He wanted to question him as a witness in a 1978 real estate transaction that John had nothing to do with. In fact, John had spoken with an investigator on the same case two years before, and had told him everything he knew about it, which apparently wasn't much. He'd never heard another word about it—until now.

For some reason, the spin became that John Zaccaro was being investigated, rather than just being called in to aid an investigation. It was clear that in the general public's mind it was all the same, and I'm sure that's what the Republicans hoped.

This was followed by a *New York* magazine item in the August 20 issue. It claimed that thirteen years before, in 1971, John's father had rented space in one of his buildings to an alleged organized crime figure. John's father had died in 1971. John sold the building in question immediately after his father's death to satisfy estate taxes. I was disgusted. What did this have to do with my running for vice president?

Finally, as an antidote to all of the poisonous accusations, John and I decided to put everything on the table—to exceed any possible concept of legal requirement in our financial disclosure. We would provide copies of tax returns, property transactions, reimbursements, gifts, and current statements of net worth. No other candidate in history had ever so publicly bared the minutiae of his or her financial affairs.

In retrospect, it was a kind of hell. We basically barricaded ourselves in our accountant's offices and started going over every detail of our financial lives. I didn't understand John's business, but now I was forced to try to cram as much information as I could about it into my brain in as short a time as possible. I was going to face a press conference concerning my disclosures, and I had to be prepared.

On Sunday I was to appear on *This Week with David Brinkley*. Late on Saturday night, I found John going through piles of old records, looking for an item of income from years ago. He was unable to find it. Exhausted, distraught, beaten down by weeks of ripping down the walls of his private life, he looked at me with overwhelming despair, and something broke in him. He began to cry. I hugged him to me and cried, too. At that moment, John Jr. passed our open door and saw us. It must have been quite a shock for him—his normally strong parents clinging to each other and bawling their eyes out. But it was his reaction to our evident distress that impressed me the most. From that night until the campaign was over, John Jr. made it a point to always be with one of us. On the rare occasions when we were home, he deferred going out with his friends to stay with his parents. It was clear that our son had taken our tears to heart, and if one of us were to ever need him, he intended to be right there.

Our frustration, panic, and exhaustion were stanched by a late-night call to our accountant. He assured us that the item was in the report, and showed us where.

The next day I appeared on *This Week with David Brinkley.* I spent most of my time going over the 1978 campaign loan, defending my taking of the spousal exemption on the congressional disclosure statements and fending off other parries at our finances. And of course, I had to defend myself for being an Italian American.

"A lot of us have grown up with a vowel at the end of our name," I said. "Just because we're Italian American, there's an immediate implication that we're connected in some way to organized crime. I find that appalling." I stared directly into the camera. "I have no words to describe my anger at someone attempting to imply that." A clear picture of Rupert Murdoch popped into my mind at that moment. His *New York Post* had so far led the charge in unfounded accusations and muckraking hearsay against John and me, although the *Philadelphia Inquirer* was doing everything it could to keep pace.

George Will, who had written a particularly nasty—and patently untrue— column in the *Washington Post* that very morning, was now sitting next to me on *This Week.* He'd had the nerve to claim that my husband didn't want to release his tax returns because he'd probably not paid very much in taxes. I turned to him and said, "Tomorrow afternoon, you're going to call me up and apologize for your column of today."

That was the high point for Sunday. The rest of the day was awash in lawyers and accountants. How much more had we paid in taxes by choosing to file separately? What was my exact voting record in Congress on matters pertaining to real estate? I was trying at the same time to absorb technical details concerning John's purchase of various properties under different corporate entities. It was chaotic. My mind was buzzing.

Monday's full disclosure showdown was to begin at 10 A.M. on the nose. The first section was to be a technical briefing, but at the last moment, the Arthur Young accountants discovered that some additional information was needed. They weren't ready to file the disclosure statements. The filing and the briefing were now put off until 1 P.M. I had until 5:30 P.M. to file the disclosure statement with the Federal Election Commission, and my accountants weren't ready. While lawyers continued to brief me for the next day's crucial press conference, I kept calling Irwin Ettinger and Charlie Reynolds of Arthur Young, exhorting them to go ahead and file, then do the briefing. But they refused. They had to have the entire package perfectly prepared if they were going to proceed. I respected that, but my stomach didn't. At 5:19 P.M., just eleven minutes before the official deadline, the disclosure statement was filed with the FEC. The accountant's technical briefing was moved to eleven-thirty the next morning, an hour and a half before my press conference was scheduled to begin.

Life is a maelstrom sometimes. No matter your good intentions, you can open the door of a pedestrian life and walk out into a tornado of massive proportions. That's what the press conference seemed like—it was excessive in the extreme. Over 250 reporters, thirty-six television cameras with their attendant crews, and scores of photographers all jammed into the ballroom at the Viscount Hotel. It appeared that a thousand news directors across the country saw my press conference as the story. I wasn't intimidated and I wasn't flattered. I wasn't daunted by the size of the assembled media coterie. I was going to go out there and answer every question as honestly and as directly as I could. My financial disclosure statement had been public for eighteen hours, and various media organizations had no doubt used that time to look for ways to tear us apart.

I was ready for a fight. I walked out to begin the press conference at 1 P.M. sharp. The sound system didn't work.

After an interminable wait standing in front of the press, I walked off the stage with a friendly shrug and a wave. I told the technician to let me know when the problem was fixed, and I'd return. Apparently the soundboard had been subjected to an overload because of the media circus, and a fuse had blown. Ten minutes later, the technician told me that he wouldn't be able to repair the board.

"Okay," I said, "set up all the individual mikes instead, and let's go."

And that's exactly what was done. After a further wait, I was finally able to go out there and hold the press conference. As I expected, the press didn't hold back. And neither did I. For well over ninety minutes I answered any and all questions asked of me. The questioning went on until it became repetitious, which is ultimately what I'd aimed for. I wanted to make sure everyone got the point: I wasn't backing away from any of this, I wasn't trying to cut people off. If I had to, I'd answer the same questions again and again, until it became clear to all who watched that there was nothing further to learn.

When it was over, I think I finally understood what it was like to be a boxer. Destructive hands are flying at you in a squared circle. Your opponent's intentions are negative. Your choice is to be beaten to the ground or to defend yourself. It is a game of human chess, brief and brutal. The press conference was long, but I felt that I gave as good as I got. And I walked out of the ring still on my feet.

George Will didn't call—first he sent roses. Then he called. "You did a superb job," he admitted.

This had been more than a test—it had been a trial by fire. The campaign regained its footing and moved on. From that time, the national press began taking my candidacy seriously, and the constant harassment about our finances seemed to die down as well.

The next day in Washington, I spoke to three thousand cheering members of the American Federation of Teachers. "Today is the first day of the rest of the campaign," I told the enthusiastic crowd. "Normally, I begin a speech by saying, 'I'm delighted to be here.' After this week I have to tell you, I'm absolutely thrilled."

The mail poured in at the rate of three thousand letters a day. I was constantly moved and humbled by the faith of the people—especially the outpouring of love and support from women. Women in their eighties and nineties wrote to say, "I never thought I'd live to see this day." An elderly woman enclosed the first campaign contribution she'd ever made—the most meaningful $2 I received.

One night, on one of my rare stays in Queens, I arrived home late and sank gratefully into the sofa cushions, kicking the pumps off my aching feet. On the table was a pile of mail, and I began idly opening the envelopes.

A letter from Greenville, Pennsylvania, marked PERSONAL, PLEASE HANDSTAMP, contained holy medals and pictures, not only for me but for my mother, my husband, and Walter Mondale. A woman from Philadelphia wrote to tell me that I had been recently enrolled in the Saint Basil League of Prayer. A note from a woman named Laura Ferraro, living in France, informed me that our grandfathers were brothers, while a Mr. Santoro let me know that my cousin Carlo Andrisani was his second cousin. A Mrs. Johnson from Brooklyn asked where she could learn about the craft of crochet embroidery, which my mother had mentioned in an interview about me. There were heartfelt, intimate messages from half-remembered neighbors, distant relatives, people I'd never known.

One letter from Florida, addressed to "The Mother of Geraldine Ferraro," read:

> Dear Lady,
>
> Congratulations! And thank you for raising Geraldine the way you did. I admire her whole heartedly. Her spunk. Her intellect. Her looks. Her loyalty and her demonstrated ideals of

> fairness. She is totally the right person for leadership. I am an old retired teacher in traction recuperating from a fall. And any time anything concerning Geraldine is in the news it lifts me up. More than I can explain. It gives me the same hope we had when FDR implemented the New Deal. I know with your daughter elected millions will have renewed hope. I hope I live long enough to see Geraldine awarded First Lady of the World.

But it was the clip from the *Miami Herald*—dateline September 16, 1984, Marcianise, Italy—that made me realize how much excitement was being poured out across the sea. Marcianise, my father's hometown, was cheering me on as one of its own. I had visited this village for the first time when I was twenty-two and had traveled through it on several other occasions. But it was only now, sitting in Queens with sore feet, that it came alive to me.

According to the article, the village had gone crazy with collective pride at the news of my nomination. More than a dozen residents interviewed referred to me as part of their family, "our Gerry." A young woman named Carla Merola said, "I get goose bumps thinking she came from Marcianise." Gaetana Piccolo, who now lived in the old Ferraro house, said how much she wished she could vote in America. I read how Mayor Piero Squeglia was planning to come to America to make me an honorary citizen of the city, how Raffaele Carrillo proudly spread out census files to prove that my grandparents had lived in the village. The names began to run together—Piccolo, Carrillo, Merola. Suddenly, in that study, surrounded by prayer medals and novenas, I felt the power of my ancestry rise up inside me; for the first time I experienced a visceral connection with my heritage. I pictured my grandmother, Maria Giuseppa, a girl in steerage, looking across the ocean toward a country she could not imagine. What would she have thought if she'd lived to witness her granddaughter's triumph, to see what her courage and forbearance had wrought?

In the midst of my modern suburban life, I had begun to think of myself as simply American, but the article, along with these letters, reminded me of the truth. These people—from Marcianise to Philadelphia—were my forebears, the ones who stood behind me whether I appreciated it or not. I was forty-nine years old and just beginning to understand who I was.

• NINE •

A VICTORY OF FAITH

I had always believed that some things in life were so sacred that no one would dare touch them. One of those was the memories a girl carried of her father. But in the ugly war zone of national politics, this too was fair game.

On October 18 I was in the air between Seattle, Washington, and Jefferson City, Missouri, when my staff gently broke the news to me that they'd been holding back all morning. Not wanting to distract me from the important foreign policy speech I was giving at the University of Washington, they'd agreed to wait until we were airborne.

Now I listened with disbelief and fury as I was told about a story that had appeared in Rupert Murdoch's *New York Post.* The story was about my father, who had been dead for forty years. Apparently, in 1944, just before his death, my father had been arrested in our hometown of Newburgh, New York, for allegedly running a numbers game. When she heard of his arrest, my mother rushed to the police station and was arrested on the spot as an accomplice—although she was just as quickly released. On the morning he was to appear in court, my father had died. The day after she buried my father, my mother was forced to appear in court to face the charges that had been brought against them. The DA asked the judge, in light of my father's death, to dismiss all charges against her, which he did.

I hadn't known. I was only eight when it happened, and my mother had been too ashamed to tell me. And all I wanted to do was speak to my mother before someone told her about the article. She had stopped reading the *Post* because of its scurrilous attacks on me, but I was afraid someone in the press might call her looking for comment, or a well-meaning friend would bring her a copy to look at.

My poor mother! How she must have suffered, keeping that bitter secret for all these years. I was haunted by the picture of her sitting alone in court the day after she buried my father. I was hurt for her that her last days with my father were anxious and fearful.

It was urgent that I speak to my mother. I convinced them to land the plane in Rapid City, South Dakota, for refueling, and I ran to a phone. With shaking fingers, I dialed her number, and I could tell by the bright tone of my mother's voice that she hadn't heard. "I love you," I blurted out forcefully. Before she could respond, I quietly told her about the story in the *Post.* She began crying. "I'm so sorry, Gerry. I should have told you when you grew up. Oh, I never thought . . ." She could barely speak through her tears. She was wracked with guilt, but so was I. My candidacy seemed to be shattering the lives of the people I loved the most. Now the world knew my mother's secret, and my father's name had been smeared.

I was in a rage by the time we landed in Jefferson City. The press was gathered, like carnivorous animals drawn to the scent of fresh meat. I stood before them with hardened eyes. "Let me say to you quite frankly that Rupert Murdoch is an individual, with all his money, with all his power, with all his connections to the White House, who does not have the worth to wipe the dirt under my mother's shoes," I said coldly.

One reporter asked me if I'd talked to my mother about it.

"Yes, I have," I replied. "I didn't ask my mother whether any of these allegations were true or not, and I don't intend to ask her."

"Did you cry when you heard the news?" someone called out. I wouldn't even dignify that. I walked past them to my waiting car. But that was the single question everyone wanted answered—did the female vice presidential candidate shed tears? The subtext of the question was plain: Did I cry? Would I cry again? Would I cry if I had to make a tough decision? Could a woman who cried be trusted with the nuclear button? I knew where they were heading, and I refused to answer, except to say, "I don't cry easily."

But alone in my hotel room, I did cry. I cried for my own lost innocence, for my father's shame—which I now believed had killed him—and for my mother's pain. I cried for the wounds my candidacy had inflicted on my husband and my children. And I cried for the sheer frustration of it all—that my message was not being heard amid the distractions. For the first time, I longed for the campaign to be over. I wanted to go home.

When I entered political life it was because I recognized that the legislative process was the vehicle for change. Economics, education, Social Security, safe streets, peace—these issues mattered to me. I was reenergized daily by the crowds that flocked to my campaign stops. They were listening; they longed for straight talk on what really mattered in their lives. I would have liked to put my arm around every grandmother in America, shake the hand of every parent. The people gave me strength. I couldn't let them down. But in a national election, the campaign trail is littered with land mines with enough explosive power to demolish talk on the issues. As the first woman to set foot on this trail, I encountered more than my share, and I tried to be philosophical about it. I told myself that the next woman would have it much easier—that I was paving the way for something better, just as my ancestors had done. Still, in an election where there were so many critical issues to be explored, I resented the sideshows.

My ethnicity and gender formed the subtext of every attack, and I was getting used to it. But I had hoped that religion would not enter the arena. This was another sacred matter, the private practice of faith.

I cherished my Catholic faith dearly. In the soulful rituals and quiet absolutions of the church, I found comfort and inspiration. Every Sunday when I sat with my family on the well-worn pews and repeated the prayers that I had said since childhood—first in Latin, now in English—the world fell away. Before God I was a humble supplicant, striving for understanding and faith—a woman whose conscience was formed around the simple moralities of life.

I never understood how any human being could challenge another's righteousness. Such judgments belonged to God, not man. I had an inherent distrust of the holier-than-thou—those who claimed to be the voice of God's will on earth. Narrow principles and rigid practices could not contain the bottomless depth of the human experience.

In part, I adopted my religious convictions from my Italian heritage. My mother's faith was extremely profound—her life one of devotion. Not a day went by when my mother didn't pray. Yet she was also an independent person, a thinking woman. She was the caretaker of her own soul. She never handed it over to the church.

I had long ago made peace with my convictions on the subject of abortion. On a personal level, I abided by my church's teachings. Abortion could not have been *my* choice. But I absolutely believed that it was a personal decision that every woman had a right to make on her own. It wasn't my place to condemn—either as a woman or as a political figure. Abortion was the law of the land, and I felt it had no place in politics.

However, since I'd first encountered abortion as a campaign issue in 1978, the debate had grown increasingly inflamed. The religious right had become a political entity, capable of delivering huge blocs of votes to the candidate that met its moral standards.

Ronald Reagan was the first antiabortion activist to inhabit the White House. Every administration appointee had to pass the abortion litmus test. His surgeon general, C. Everett Koop, was an inflammatory antiabortionist, often comparing abortion to the Holocaust. We knew from the outset that abortion would be a campaign issue.

However, the blurring of distinction between church and state was very troubling. It distressed me greatly when Archbishop John O'Connor of New York stepped over the line. This was a bishop, in my home state, holding a televised news conference to say: "I do not see how a Catholic in good conscience can vote for an individual expressing himself or herself as favoring abortion." A reporter asked the archbishop if New York governor Mario Cuomo and other pro-choice Catholic politicians should be excommunicated, and he didn't reject the idea. The following day, New York papers blared headlines about the possible excommunication of pro-choice public officials.

Excommunication is the most devastating condemnation the Catholic Church can give. It requires a sin so grievous that one is severed from connection with the church. That the archbishop could even leave the matter open made me physically ill, and it placed yet another stress on my mother's iron heart.

On Sunday, I was shaking as I approached the altar to receive Holy Communion. I had visions of being denied, of being thrown from the church.

"Body of Christ," the priest intoned as he offered me the Communion host.

"Amen," I replied, receiving it.

"Be strong, Gerry, be strong," he added.

The Archbishop continued his attacks. At a September 8 news conference, he produced a letter from Catholics for a Free Choice that I'd signed—along with two other Catholic congressmen—while in Congress. Waving the pamphlet, the archbishop claimed that "Geraldine Ferraro has said some things about abortion relevant to Catholic teachings which are not true . . . what has been said is wrong—it's wrong." The archbishop was the arbiter of church teachings, and I had no intention of debating him on the subject. As a matter of fact, my biggest problem was that I couldn't recall ever making a statement that said anything about Catholic teachings. It wasn't easy, but I got my staff to track the archbishop down and get him on the phone for me. When I was later asked about the conversation by the press, I said it was a cordial exchange—but it wasn't.

"This is Geraldine Ferraro," I began. "I've been asked by the press to respond to your statement that I've said the church is *not* monolithic in its stand on abortion. I'm a little concerned, because I don't remember ever making that statement."

"You did make that statement," the archbishop retorted icily.

We went back and forth until he pointed out an undated letter I'd signed. I had no recollection of it, but I promised him that I'd find a copy and look at it. I also reminded the archbishop that I'd always said that I did understand the church's teachings and what they were, and I'd always said the church and I disagreed on this particular issue. We left it at that and said our good-byes.

When I finally dug up the two-year-old cover letter, it turned out to be part of an invitation to Catholic legislators for a breakfast meeting sponsored by Catholics for a Free Choice. A professor of theology and ethics was invited to speak about abortion, as well as the Washington correspondent for a Catholic newspaper and a pollster with statistics on recent abortion opinions. Buried in the letter was this paragraph: "It [the briefing] will show us that the Catholic position on abortion is not monolithic and that there can be a range of personal and political responses to the issue."

I knew what the church *taught*. The letter said the Catholic *position* was not monolithic. Had I inadvertently presumed to speak for the teachings of the church? Not at all, but like many prominent Catholic leaders and theologians—along with some bishops, nuns, brothers, and priests—I did presume to disagree with the specific dictates of the Vatican.

A few days after the archbishop's attack on me, Catholics began coming out in droves wherever I spoke, carrying signs saying NUNS FOR FERRARO, and CATHOLICS FOR FERRARO. It was very encouraging. And, of course, the antiabortion forces really stepped up their attacks wherever I campaigned, waving signs proclaiming THOU SHALT NOT KILL—ABORTION IS MURDER, and MONDALE-FERRARO FOR INFANT GENOCIDE.

Also a few days after my conversation with the archbishop, there was a huge rally in largely Catholic Scranton, Pennsylvania. The antiabortion forces promised to show up in force and make their feelings known. Twenty-five thousand people were jammed into one block on Wyoming Avenue in Scranton. The police had done a tremendous job of separating the opposing sides but could do nothing to keep down the deafening roar of the crowd. The hecklers were going to make it hard for me to speak.

I decided to tackle it head-on. I wanted a chance to address the separation of church and state, to address the archbishop of New York's attack, and to make sure that my position was clear. I walked up to the podium and began speaking. Loudly.

"I don't want to be misunderstood," I said. "Religious leaders and other citizens should speak out forcefully on matters that they feel are important. I respect their point of view. I encourage open debate, and question no person's sincerity. People are doing their duty as citizens and church officials when they speak out.

"But I also have my duty as a public official. When I take my oath of office, I accept the charge of serving all the people of every faith, not just some of the people of my own faith. I also swear to uphold the Constitution of the United States, which guarantees freedom of religion. These are my public duties. And in carrying them out, I cannot, and I will not, seek to impose my own religious views on others. If ever my conscience or my religious views prevented me from carrying out those duties to the best of my ability, then I would resign my office before I'd betray the public trust."

The crowd erupted into predictably partisan cheers, but I felt strong and good. A lot of the Italians and Catholics in Scranton seemed to like me, although the local bishop, Scranton's Bishop Timlin, tore into my pro-choice position.

Meanwhile, Reagan and Bush continued to run as God's ticket. The televangelist Reverend Jerry Falwell declared Reagan-Bush "God's instrument for rebuilding America." Senator Paul Laxalt of Nevada, general chairman of Reagan's campaign, sent out literature to forty-five thousand ministers calling Reagan supporters "leaders under God's authority." Reagan himself crossed the line as well, accusing those who opposed his call for a constitutional amendment permitting prayer in school of being intolerant of religion.

In the midst of all of this politics and piety there came a further attempt at disparagement—by the Coalition for Italo-American Associations. I was scheduled to speak at the first annual black tie dinner of the coalition in New York. The dinner was arranged by Republican senator Al D'Amato and state Reagan-Bush coordinator Charles Gargano.

Originally, a scheduling conflict made it unlikely that I'd be able to attend the dinner, until the Republicans began spreading the word that Vice President Bush would be in town for the dinner. It was also hinted that Bush was more supportive of Italian Americans than was Ferraro. Heavy-handed? Ridiculous? Of course. But it aggravated me, and it worked.

Lured by my righteous anger, I fell right into the trap the Republicans had so carefully prepared for me. I changed my schedule to accommodate the dinner, only to discover that Bush wouldn't be there. It would be just me and the archbishop on the dais together.

When I rose to speak to the coalition and its guests, I tried to appeal to the ethnic pride that spread far beyond my candidacy. But the crowd at the dinner, following the lead of the somber prelate who sat glumly to my right, seemed little interested in the national support I'd garnered in every Italian American community across the country but my own. It didn't matter—it was clear who was sitting out there that evening, and they weren't Democrats.

It didn't end there, of course. I'd been invited to march in Philadelphia's Columbus Day parade. But Cardinal John Krol, the conservative Philadelphia archbishop who'd delivered the invocation the evening of Reagan's renomination at the Republican convention, announced that if I was allowed to march in the parade, he'd pull all the Catholic kids out. Krol said that I didn't represent the Catholic community and I didn't represent the Italian American community. So I pulled out. I had no intention of being divisive in a community that I cared so deeply for, but I thought it was sad. It turned out there was going to be plenty to be sad about.

For four months I was the most recognizable Italian American in the country, but it didn't buy me much respect in New York. The day after I pulled out of the Philadelphia parade, I was placed in the back of New York City's Columbus Day parade with other members of Congress. Sophia Loren was the grand marshal that year. But it was clear that if the Italian American vice presidential candidate had been a man, a way would have been found to change the marching order. It turned out that the Columbus Day parade was being run that year by Charles Gargano, the same Charles Gargano from the coalition dinner.

My defenders those days were few and far between. Finally, syndicated columnist Richard Reeves wrote, "The stoning of Geraldine Ferraro in the public square goes on and on, and no one steps forward to help or protest—not even one of her kind. Especially her own kind. The sons of Italy and fathers of the Roman Catholic Church are silent or are too busy reaching for bigger rocks. Other women seem awed and intimidated by the charges and innuendo: Heresy! Mafia! Men are putting women in their place."

Reeves's conclusion boded ill for the future of our nation. "If Geraldine Ferraro is stoned without defenders, she will be only the first to fall. The stones will always be there, piled high, ready for the next Italian, the next Catholic, the next woman."

As the end of the campaign grew near, I realized that we weren't going to win. Polls showed us eighteen points behind, and it seemed to be a gap that wouldn't close. If anything, the margin energized us even more. I went at the relentless schedule with renewed vigor. The crowds in those final weeks were the largest we had seen, and the most passionate. Mondale and I kept hammering away—about the economy, about fairness, about the arms race. The response was so overwhelming, you'd never have guessed we were so far behind in the polls.

I made sure that my last stop of the 1984 campaign was Marymount College. I felt very subdued when I arrived there that evening. I hadn't wanted to end this very special campaign in some hotel ballroom or airport courtesy lounge. I wanted a small event with my family around me. Classmates, former teachers, and other friends who had meant so much to me filled the audience. But more than anything, I wanted the opportunity to honor my mother.

As I took the stage, I felt an incredible sense of peace. I had practiced this speech endlessly, almost memorizing it. It was important to me that I not break down and begin crying during this, my last campaign stop.

"Tonight we come to the end of a journey without precedent in our nation's history," I began. "Tomorrow the nation votes. This is the clearest choice in fifty years."

I pointed out that my education had given me an incalculable advantage in life, but what had really made the difference was my parents. They believed their children should have a better chance than they of achieving the American dream, regardless of the cost to them. And then I told the audience about my mother.

"Because of her sacrifice, I had the privilege to attend this college. Because of that dedication, I am what I am today. And tonight, I would like to say to her from the bottom of my heart: Thank you for everything." I had avoided looking at my mother until then, and when I did, all of my emotional control began washing away. My voice breaking, my eyes filling with tears, I then said to my mother, "I hope you are proud of me. I will always be proud of you."

I looked away from her. I had to if I was going to continue speaking. Fighting to regain control, I took a deep breath and went on.

"Ours was perhaps the first generation of American women free to choose our own careers. Against that background of achievement and progress, every woman of my generation has felt discrimination. All of us know women our age who were denied opportunities they had earned. And despite the progress we've seen in our lifetime, we want for our daughters more freedom to develop their talents than we had.

"Let's be clear about this," I continued. "Sexism has no place in American life. Racism has no right to a home in our land. Ageism has no role in our values. And if there's one thing my candidacy stands for, it is that Americans should be able to reach as far as our dreams will take us."

And finally I was able to speak about my family. "The voters decide in a few hours. But yesterday, today, and tomorrow, my concern is also for my family. In the last three months, my children and my husband were my mainstays, just as they have been for the last twenty-four years. They have encouraged me, comforted me, loved me, and backed me all the way. I couldn't have done this without them.

"It hasn't always been easy, but it's been worth it for all of us. Even if this moment were frozen in time, this campaign would still have made a difference. My candidacy has said to women: The doors of opportunity are opening. And for me, life can never be the same, because I have been touched by the support, the love, and the goodwill of men and women all over America."

And then I went on to exhort the crowd to vote for Walter Mondale. The 1984 presidential campaign was over, and the choice was now up to the people of America.

"Noi poniamo i nostri sogni nei figli—e con fede in Dio, lavoriamo affinchè questi sogni si realizzino," I proclaimed, my voice rising to form the melodic Italian syllables. "We place our dreams in our children, and with faith in God we work toward the realization of those dreams."

• TEN •

UNFINISHED BUSINESS

A half century had gone by in a flash, and I was suddenly on the brink of fifty. As I sat on the beach on the island of Saint Croix, where John and I went to rest and recover after the bruising pace of the election, I pondered the last six years. I felt as if this were the first time since 1978 that I'd drawn a full breath. My entry into political life occurred at a moment in our national history when social, economic, and cultural issues had become more sharply defined than ever before through the prism of gender. The concerns that I faced as a woman, a wife, a mother, and a daughter were mirrored in the concerns of my constituents. When I was first elected to Congress, the social climate had undergone a metamorphosis. The vital issues had become more practical than ideological, more real than rhetorical: domestic abuse, day care, elder care, job discrimination, welfare, education, teenage pregnancy, abortion—all of the things that really happened in life. I could speak to the issues because they were the stuff of my own life.

I'd rubbed elbows with the real world. I was at home in my district, and I discovered a second home on the Hill during my time in Congress.

Running for the vice presidency on a national ticket was exhilarating, thrilling, and completely beyond my expected realm of experience. It would take some time to fully comprehend the significance of those brief months. I was constantly being asked, "Was it worth it?" Of course it was worth it! I was the first woman to run on a national ticket. It had been a tremendous honor, and it had been a very humbling experience, as well. My candidacy was a benchmark moment for women. No matter what anyone thought of me personally, or of the Mondale-Ferraro ticket, my candidacy had flung open the last door barring equality—and that door led straight to the Oval Office. From the time I was chosen until the night we lost, we changed the lives and aspirations of more young girls than we ever could have imagined the night I accepted the nomination in San Francisco.

My position on the ticket also broke an entrenched ethnic barrier. For more than a century, immigrant Italians and their American-born offspring had made tremendous contributions to the nation's prosperity—as laborers, entrepreneurs, small business owners, and community leaders. They had fought and died in wars. Their patriotism was unrivaled. Nevertheless, biases had woven a tight web around the country's consciousness, and those biases had effectively kept Italian Americans from the highest corridors of power. Fears of inclusion were based in part on superstition, and in part on mistrust. How ironic that a population that had been so essential to America's advancement in the twentieth century would still be deemed foreign. But America had always been this way, filled with ethnic divisions as well as racial, religious, and class restraints. My nomination served as an announcement to all Italian Americans that hereafter no opportunity would be closed to them. Twenty-four years before, John F. Kennedy had finally broken through the Irish

American barrier, which of course included the additional burden of being a Roman Catholic. Now, at last, Italian American Catholics were in the game.

I felt strong and confident when I addressed the enthusiastic crowds across the span of the nation. I witnessed thousands of women cheering, shouting, and stamping their feet in sheer exuberant joy. Mothers, daughters, and granddaughters were hugging one another and dancing in the aisles. The warmth and energy of the well-wishers, the prayers that people were saying for me, the thousands of letters of encouragement—all of it was a big part of what kept me going.

I also had to deal with the stereotypes at every turn, which became frustrating as the campaign wore on. America was ready to see a woman on a national ticket, but there was a leaden bloc of those who simply didn't believe that a woman could take the pressure, and they were intent on using their weight to drag me to the bottom, if necessary. Couldn't take the pressure? They didn't know me, and obviously they'd never met my mother! I grew weary of the constant discussions about whether a woman had the mettle it took to push the nuclear button. And often I felt goaded by the press, as if ultimately we were still children on a playground—the boys thinking if they teased me hard enough I'd finally burst into tears and run away.

The breakthrough that my candidacy represented for women was tainted by the inability of the press to allow me equal standing with the men. My being a separate entity from, and independent of, my husband was a foreign concept to the media. No male candidate had ever gone through such a scrutiny of his wife's finances and business dealings.

While I was tremendously buoyed by the support of large numbers of proud Italian Americans, and warmed by the sight of jubilant celebrations in my father's hometown in Italy, I was also hurt by the failure of the Italian American community to rise up against the barrage of charges and innuendos that were leveled against John and me—the persistent rumors of our ties to organized crime. Was the silence motivated by fear? I think so. There still exists a hesitancy in some segments of the Italian American community—a feeling that we've still not been fully accepted. This was the old way of responding to bias, the way practiced by my grandparents. Remain silent, don't rock the boat, keep to oneself, try to be invisible, try to blend in and not be noticed. One of the great keys to being an American was to assimilate. I think it surprised me that as a community, our fear of being shamed, singled out, was still greater than our confidence in being fully accepted Americans. My mother's old admonishment "People will talk" became a reality in the campaign. And the Italian American community bowed its head in shame instead of fighting back. When, I wondered, were we going to really speak up—as the Jewish community had, as African Americans had—and insist on no longer being marred by crude stereotypes? The attacks against my family hurt not only us. They hurt every citizen whose name ended with a vowel.

Long before I became a lawyer, I'd dreamed of being a journalist. Perhaps I was idealistic then, but it seemed like a meaningful vocation. Yet dealing with the press during the campaign was more like being cornered by a pack of hungry dogs. They were far less interested in what I had to say about the life-and-death issues facing the nation than they were about what I was wearing, how I looked that day, whether or not I cried, and what was happening in my marriage.

After the election, I learned from my father's relatives in Italy that the media fever had invaded the small town of Marcianise, to the horror of its residents. The town was bursting with pride, but they weren't so happy when the television network trucks started parking on their narrow streets. My relatives, who were quite comfortable with their quiet lives, were appalled when the paparazzi started following them. My cousin Maria Tartaglione told me that an Italian magazine even followed her family on vacation to the isle of Ponza, where they tried to shoot revealing pictures of sixteen-year-old Sonja as she sunbathed on the beach. A number of fabrications started appearing in Italian magazines and tabloids. There were rumors that the family was angry about my success and all the attention it had garnered them. There were rumors that pretty young Sonja was going to be a candidate for Miss Italy, when in fact she had refused all offers of further exploitation.

The press was disenchanted with the truth, which was really quite simple and not very interesting. My extended family in Marcianise was thrilled with my candidacy in 1984, proud that "the serious young woman" with such strong ties to their town had become such a prominent political figure in America.

I went into the campaign ready to wage a passionate fight on the major issues facing our nation. The Republicans had other plans. I found myself constantly distracted—ambushed, really—by relatively trivial personal issues and questions that had nothing whatsoever to do with the real battle at hand. It was discouraging. I had been raised by the nuns and by my mother to use my head and my heart to succeed, but for once these weren't enough.

Because of my candidacy, each of the people I loved the most in the world had suffered. John, the children, my mother—they all assured me that it was worth it. Whatever their personal hurts, they saw them as part of a contribution to history—mine, theirs, the nation's.

As I sat on the beach with John, baking in the tropical sun of Saint Croix, I let the heat and the quiet melt away the tension of endless days and nights that had been spent on the road campaigning. The roar of the crowds was replaced by the gentle lapping of the waves on the warm sand. I considered everything that had happened, and I wondered about all that was ahead. I finally had time to take stock of my life.

* * *

In 1985, the same year I was to turn fifty, John and I would celebrate twenty-five years of marriage. During the campaign, there were frequent rumors circulating in the tabloids that our marriage was on the rocks, that we were about to get divorced. I am told that Frank Sinatra, watching us on television during the campaign, even commented, "As soon as this is over, he's going to divorce that broad!" I guess some people were unable to believe that a marriage could survive such a harsh test, such a minute examination. But in many ways we grew closer as a result of our tribulations. John reinforced the true meaning of love and loyalty. Not a word of blame ever crossed his lips, even during the darkest of times. On many occasions, I would be a thousand miles away in some hotel, and I'd call John and hear the strain in his voice. There was one period when the worst of the allegations were making headlines, and he became deeply depressed. I was far away on the campaign trail, and there was little I could do. My reassurances by phone sounded hollow. "Things are going to get better," I'd say with forced cheer, hoping to fool him into believing that none of it was bothering me and none of it should bother him. "They're only getting worse," he'd quietly say.

I was in a hotel room in Nashville, and after I hung up the phone that night, I got down on my knees and prayed. I wanted to give strength to my husband, and the only way it seemed possible at that moment was through God. Usually it was my mother who held the fort when it came to prayer. My mother's constant in life was the novenas, rosaries, votive candles, and supplications to the saints that formed the basis of her faith. I hadn't knelt beside my bed and prayed since I was a little girl. But now I did. "God, please help us," I begged. "Help us get through this." I knew we wouldn't be able to do it on our own.

The next day John's voice sounded better. "We've been through a lot and we're going to get through this, too," he said. I breathed a sigh of thankful relief. We'd be okay.

After the 1984 campaign was over, we still had each other, and that was the important thing. We decided to symbolize the strength of our love and commitment. On February 10, 1985, John and I stood together before a priest, in Our Lady Queen of Mercy Church, and renewed our wedding vows in front of our family and friends. The tears that flowed that day had nothing to do with sorrow or regret. Only joy.

I had one more piece of unfinished business to take care of in the months following the election. My father's death. The *New York Post* article had implied that there was a mystery surrounding how and when he died—and that there might have been a cover-up. The *Post* reported that my father's death notice in the newspaper had been altered at the request of the undertaker. This raised speculation that perhaps other details had been altered as well. Unfortunately, the *Post* noted, the doctor who had attended my father had died many years ago, so there was no way of finding out exactly how he had died.

My father's last seconds of life were forever seared in my memory. I could still visualize the way he looked at me before he lay back on the bed and died. I could hear my mother's voice murmuring—"Your father has gone to heaven. He waited for you to come in." But try as I might, I could not recall any details beyond that shocking moment.

Three months after the election, I got in my car and made the sixty-mile drive to Newburgh. I needed to find some answers. I didn't mention the trip to my mother, as it would have upset her.

It had been forty years since I had stepped foot in the town of my birth. When my parents had moved to Newburgh, it had been a bustling town. But now this home of immigrant dreams and prosperity had changed. It had grown somewhat dilapidated, worn and gray. The sluggish economy had taken its toll here. Jobs were scarce, and Newburgh was searching for a new direction.

Mr. Colonie, the undertaker who had been my father's friend and had made the arrangements for his burial, was still alive. I went to see him at the big old white house he had lived in since I could remember, with the funeral parlor on the ground floor. Mr. Colonie was quite elderly by this time, but his mind was sharp and his memory clear. He remembered my father's death as if it were yesterday. "The reporter from the *Post* made a mistake," he told me. "The time of your father's death hadn't been altered—the date of the funeral had been changed."

He explained that my father had died on a holiday weekend—Memorial Day—and the cemetery had needed extra time to prepare the grave. It baffled me that the reporter could have made this error, especially since he'd used it as the platform for his conspiracy theory. Surely there must have been something else.

"Isn't it a shame that the doctor who took care of my father died so long ago?" I said wistfully. "He could have set things straight with the reporter."

Mr. Colonie raised an eyebrow. "But Dr. Steinthal only died two weeks ago," he said.

I was stunned. "You mean he was alive when the reporter visited?"

"Yes. In fact, I'm pretty sure he talked to the newspaper." Mr. Colonie suggested that I go over to the doctor's house and speak with his housekeeper. She might remember something.

Indeed she did. "The reporter interviewed Dr. Steinthal," she said. "The doctor told him your father had a heart condition, and he'd treated him for it the night before he died. The doctor signed your father's death certificate."

I was relieved to know the truth, but I also felt numb. I understood that the *New York Post* wasn't a fan of mine, but would this reporter have deliberately lied about what he knew, seeking to create the impression of a mysterious death? I didn't want to believe it, but I could find no other explanation. The reporter had spoken to Dr.

Steinthal yet had claimed that the doctor was dead and thus unavailable for corroboration of the facts. When later confronted, the reporter admitted that he had interviewed the doctor.

I know that many people believe that politics is inherently a dirty business. But I believe that the political process is about something else, about lifting people up rather than looking for ways to tear them apart. What the *Post* did was reprehensible. It probably made no difference in the outcome of the election, but it caused great suffering for people who didn't deserve to suffer. I wondered how the reporter from the *Post* felt about *his* mother? I wondered if he would think it a small thing to cause her the amount of pain and heartbreak he had caused *mine.*

Ever so gradually, our life returned to normal. Reporters stopped dogging our every step. In April, I accepted an invitation to speak to a European conference in Copenhagen, Denmark, on the future of women in politics and management. I used the opportunity to talk frankly about the critical matters that faced our nations—the budget deficit, free trade, and arms control.

"If ever there were two continents whose fortunes were linked in history, they would be North America and Europe," I told the assembly. "If ever two peoples had worked together with huge success, they would be the peoples of America and Europe.

"Don't forget that when my father and thirty-five million other Europeans set out from this side of the ocean to journey to the other side, they could have moved to any country on earth—but they chose the United States. My father came to America not because it was so different from Europe, but because in many important ways, it was similar to Europe—with the same values, the same culture, the same faith in democracy, and the same love of freedom."

It was true. I thought it was time that we shifted our focus away from all the areas that divided us, and instead focused on all of the commonalities that brought us together. Looking to the final years of the century, I hoped that we could begin building bridges that would further cement the bonds of global accord and cooperation.

John Jr. was studying for a semester in Florence, so John and I flew to Italy to visit him on our way home. I had not been there since 1980, when I'd been part of a fact-finding mission sent by President Carter to survey the damage of a massive earthquake that had struck southern Italy. The earthquake—*terremoto*—had measured 7.2 on the Richter scale and left at least three thousand people dead. The earthquake's devastation was enhanced by its location, as hundreds of towns clung tenaciously to the mountainous terrain of the south—tiny villages like my grandmother's home, Terranova, which sat precariously atop winding mountain roads. As our delegation flew in a government helicopter above the countryside to survey the damage, I was struck by the patchwork of zigzagging roads below. It was as if they had been squeezed from a toothpaste tube.

Our chopper touched down in many of the towns, and we viewed the wreckage. Buildings that had stood for centuries were rubble. Weeks after the quake, they were still digging people out. Before the disaster, these towns had already been very poor. I'll never forget one mountaintop town. The church had been destroyed during Mass, and it had been filled with many of the villagers. As I stood and watched workmen digging for bodies, a young girl came up to me. She was dressed in black, and tears were streaming down her cheeks. She said that her entire family had been killed in the church except her, and now she had no one. I put my arms around her, and we stood together for a long time. She was only fourteen, and an orphan. I couldn't imagine the pain of having no one.

In 1985, my mother celebrated her eightieth birthday. On that day, she hugged me and said, "Gerry, this is the best time of my life."

What she meant was that she didn't have to worry about money, and she no longer had to work. Her expectations were so humble. It took so little to make her happy. It was a lesson for me, who had always wanted so much, whose expectations had always been so great.

My mother kept teaching me valuable lessons. I realized that many people were just like her. They measured happiness in small ways—food on the table, a safe place to live, the love of a family. In her final years, my mother was still reminding me of what was really important.

It made me happy to have the resources to make sure that she was comfortable in her later years. But as I thought about it, her remark made me very sad. Imagine feeling that your eighties were the best time of your life. Imagine having to wait *eighty years* for a feeling of contentment and security. My mother was bent over with osteoporosis, an elderly widow living alone. *This* was the best time of her life?

The summer after the vice presidential campaign our family resumed spending weekends on Fire Island. Often, my mother would join us, but on one particular weekend, she had remained in Queens. That weekend, my friend Madeleine Albright was visiting.

The phone rang at 2 A.M. Sunday morning. It was my mother's neighbor, saying that an ambulance had been called. My mother had been taken ill. The ferries to and from Fire Island had stopped running for the night, so I woke my son and asked him to take me to the mainland in his small speedboat. By then, everyone was up. Madeleine insisted on going with me, in spite of my protests, so we made the trip to Queens together.

When I arrived at the hospital, I found my mother in the emergency room. She looked ashen faced and tiny, and she was on a respirator. A doctor was standing by her bedside.

"Your mother has emphysema," he told me very seriously.

"Emphysema?" It was the last thing I'd expected. "How in God's name did my mother get emphysema? She doesn't smoke." I looked at my mother. She shrugged guiltily, and held her fingers up in a smoking gesture.

I stared at her openmouthed. "You smoke? But Mom, we both quit smoking years ago." Well, I had quit smoking back in 1968, and I urged my mother to quit too. I knew it was bad for her health, but I also told her I didn't want the kids exposed to smoking. And she agreed. But for all those years, she'd been smoking behind my back. The worst part of it was that every single person in my family—and my office—was in collusion with her to keep it a secret from me. She smoked when she was at Fire Island with the kids, and she'd say, "Don't tell your mother." They kept her secret. She smoked around my brother, Carl. She smoked around my husband. She smoked when she volunteered in my congressional office. She said to my staff, "You tell my daughter, I'm going to be very mad." No one said a word.

Now I looked at her sitting in the bed and I threw up my hands. "Mom, what is this? You always used to say how terrible it was when kids were sneaking around on their parents. But look—you've been sneaking around on me!"

Of course, she couldn't answer because of the respirator, but later she told me, "I'm sorry, Gerry. I wasn't going to fight with you on this. I wasn't going to say get off my back. But it was my one entertainment."

I softened when she said that. What could I say? Would I dare to chide my mother for her simple pleasure? No way. But now it was serious. "Tell me you're going to stop now," I said.

"I've got no choice," she said as if she were saying good-bye to an old friend. Certainly I sympathized, remembering what a terrible time I'd had quitting that year after John's brother, Frank, died.

After this incident, I bought an oxygen machine for her apartment so she would never have to be afraid again. If she was having trouble breathing, she could turn on the tank, put on the mask , and receive emphysema-relieving oxygen. Increasingly I began to experience the typical midlife role reversal, where I was becoming my mother's parent.

It's very hard to watch a parent age. There's a point when it hits you all at once, I think. Although aging is a gradual process, you don't really see it until it has occurred. My mother was always so vibrant, so capable of moving mountains. It was easy not to see the signs of aging. But one day I looked at her and was startled at how frail she was. I guess I began to hover a bit too much then, because she finally said, "Oh, Gerry, I'm going to live to be one hundred and fifty. Don't baby me."

I wished that she would spend more time taking care of herself and less time focusing on me, but after a lifetime of giving, she didn't know how to do that. I was still the center of her universe. But I wanted people to know about her. I was eager to find tangible ways to honor her. She had always been happy to live in the shadow of my achievements, yet she herself had achieved so much.

In September 1985, we dedicated the Antonetta Ferraro Residence in Far Rockaway, Queens, under the auspices of the Catholic Guardian Society. The residence would house fourteen developmentally disabled young men and women, offering them opportunities for education and employment that had never been available before. For the dedication, Governor Mario Cuomo wrote, "By choosing to honor Mrs. Ferraro, you pay homage to one of Queens County's finest and most loyal citizens. Her spirit and warmth touches everyone who meets her."

My mother was becoming a celebrity in her own right. She appeared as a guest of honor at fund-raisers for the residence, and she glowed with pride at having her name affiliated with such important work. In many ways, she was viewed by others as a symbol. Her struggles after the death of my father were now seen as valiant efforts not only to survive, but to provide opportunities for her children and for future generations. The following year she was honored by the Displaced Homemakers Network—a movement that had been started to represent the millions of women who were forced back into low-paying jobs following a spouse's death or disability, or in the event of divorce. In honoring my mother, the organization called her "one of the movement's own success stories."

It was incredibly gratifying to see my mother acknowledged. In some small way it was a means of paying her back—for her hard work and unflagging faith in me. I hoped that the joy she experienced in receiving these accolades would add years to her life.

I was constantly aware of how vulnerable the elderly are. I saw the fragility of age reflected in my mother and in my mother-in-law. Rose Zaccaro had been walking to church one day when a young punk ran up to her, pushed her to the ground, and grabbed her purse. There was nothing much in the purse— maybe a couple of dollars. But the impact of the assault, both physical and psychological, was great.

Eventually, the combined scourges of the emphysema and advanced osteoporosis made it necessary for my mother to use a wheelchair. I hired a lovely young Japanese college student to take my mother on her errands several times a week.

On one of these excursions, they stopped at a neighborhood green market to buy some fruit. As my mother picked up a tomato to judge its ripeness, the store owner began shouting at her furiously. "Put down the tomato," he screamed. "Stop touching the fruit!" My mother was mortified. She left the store without buying anything and refused to return.

When I finally learned of the incident several days later, I was boiling mad. How dare the grocer treat an elderly woman with such disrespect? My mother had earned the right to squeeze the damned fruit whenever she wanted. I went to her apartment and announced, "We're going to the market."

"Now, Gerry," she said, "I don't want to cause any trouble. Just let it go."

But I refused. I wheeled my mother down to the market. When we came in, the grocer looked at me with my mother. I saw that he instantly recognized who I was. I wheeled my mother over to the fruit and said, "Pick out anything you want." I handed her melons, plums, peaches, and tomatoes. I let her squeeze them all, until she had made her choices. Then I wheeled her to the front counter. The grocer weighed everything and rang it up. As I paid, I looked him in the eye and said, "My mother likes to buy her produce here." The grocer nodded. I continued, pointedly. "And she likes to pick it out herself."

His face reddened. "Of course, of course," he said hurriedly. "I'll take good care of her."

"That would be nice," I said as I handed the bags to my mother. I knew I was throwing my weight around, but it was for a good cause. My mother was going to maintain her dignity—no matter what I had to do.

In the last year of my mother's life, I spent as much time with her as I could. Every Tuesday I took off from work and we'd go shopping and have lunch. When the weather was warmer, we'd get ice cream cones and go sit on a bench in the park. We talked as we never had before, about the past, about our years apart, about my father. I had started to work on this book, and I was hungry for any stories she could tell me.

"What was it like when you were pregnant with me?" I asked.

"I was never sick a day in my life with you," she said, smiling. "But I couldn't sleep. I hadn't been able to sleep since Gerard died. So I went to the doctor and he gave me some sleeping medicine. I finished that bottle and went back for more. He didn't want to give it to me. He said, 'You're pregnant.' I said, 'What has that got to do with the baby?' He said the baby gets what you eat and drink. So I didn't want it. I stayed up half the night when I was pregnant with you."

In this way, my mother painted tiny portraits of our family life. She told me that she didn't have prenatal care with any of her children. She recalled how Carl loved me from the beginning, but our relationship was very argumentative. When Carl would torment me after my father died, my mother would tell him to stop, saying, "The little girl has lost her father"—as if Carl had not. She confessed to me one day that after my father died, she had planned to move with us to Marcianise and raise us with his family, but she changed her mind because we were in good schools.

Once I commented on how different our relationship was from the one she had with her mother. "It was different, then," she replied. "My mother had so many children and so many worries. She saw I could take care of myself; it was one less worry for her. But she was a wonderful woman. People used to see her coming down the street and smile. Everyone loved my momma."

Donna was getting married in October, and my mother and I were both very excited. Unbeknownst to me, she arranged for our family friend Sister Jean De Sales to take her shopping. She spent hours choosing Donna a collection of delicate lingerie for her bridal shower.

My mother wanted to look her best at the wedding, but her hip had become so misshapen from the osteoporosis that she could no longer buy dresses off the rack. And she could no longer physically endure the tedious process of trying on clothes. So I went to Saks, Bendel's, and Lord & Taylor and picked up five or six outfits which she would try on at home. I would return those that weren't selected. She finally settled on a two-piece fuchsia suit. I had a dressmaker come in and alter the skirt so that it fit perfectly and minimized the irregularity.

At the wedding reception, she glowed. Seeing her with Donna, I thought I had never seen her look so happy, so alive. The woman whose primary goal in life had been to see her daughter married and settled—"taken care of"—was watching her daughter's daughter do the very same thing.

Antonetta Ferraro was unable to dance at the reception, but to judge by the sparkle in her eyes, her heart was dancing to every measure of music that was played.

• ELEVEN •

Antonetta's Vision

There comes a time in every child's life when you finally are orphaned. My time was coming, but I kept myself so busy doing everything that I could to extend my mother's life, I blinded myself to the reality that she was failing.

When she called me on Thanksgiving Day and said she wasn't going to join us for dinner, I was more annoyed than concerned. My mother could sometimes get a little ornery, a little stubborn. She'd tell me to leave her alone—"Don't bother me." I had come to interpret such behavior as a roundabout way of getting attention, and that's what I figured she was doing now. When she said she wasn't feeling well, I dismissed her protests. We were going to John's mother's house for dinner, and occasionally a little rivalry would pop up. So I kept trying to talk her into joining us, but she wouldn't budge. She was adamant. I thought to myself, Oh, Ma. . . . , but I tried to keep my frustration in check. It wasn't worth making her feel bad about not coming. "Okay, we're going. We'll stop by after."

John and I and the kids brought her turkey and all the trimmings later that day, and she perked right up. We sat around and talked for a couple of hours, and her face was animated with pleasure. She loved her grandchildren, and it showed. Any previous annoyance I may have felt disappeared. I was just relieved that whatever she was feeling earlier had passed, and happy that she was enjoying Thanksgiving with her grandkids, John, and me.

That night the phone rang, and my mother's voice was thin and trembling on the other end of the line. I glanced at the clock. It was ten-thirty. My mother normally wouldn't have called me at that hour unless a tornado had moved through her apartment. "Gerry, I need you to come over and help me. I'm not feeling so good," she said, and this time I believed her. I rushed over. She was sitting up in a chair covered in a cold sweat, her face a white ashen blue, heaving in air from her oxygen machine. She didn't want to go to the hospital, so we sat together that night, alternately dozing as we listened to the whispering sound of the oxygen and her labored breathing. We held hands for hours—her tiny cold hands engulfed by mine as I tried to fill her with whatever warmth I could muster. At some point, I remember thinking, *I'm going to lose my mother.*

By early morning, my mother's eyes had grown pained and rheumy. Although she was breathing a bit more comfortably, it was clear that her condition wasn't improving. I called her doctor and was able to reach him immediately. Dr. Filardi was a wonderful, compassionate man. He wasn't a big fan of hospitalization. In fact, he'd always tried to do everything he could to keep my mother out of the hospital. A woman my mother's age, with her brittle bones and her weak heart, could quickly grow worse if she was suddenly confined to a hospital bed. But now, given the circumstances, he said she needed to be brought in immediately.

Just getting my mother to the hospital took a lot out of her, and by the time she arrived, she was having a terrible time breathing. It was while checking into the hospital on this occasion that she made the judgment on her life—"Big deal, huh?"—that was to make such a tremendous impact on me.

The doctors decided to intubate my mother, and they hooked her up to a respirator. It was a shocking thing to see my tiny mother strapped into this horrible contraption. Sedated so she wouldn't fight against the gagging intrusion of the tube down her throat, she looked like a helpless little girl. There was nothing I could do. I sat beside her bed and listened to the steady pulse of the machine giving my mother breath. I clutched one of her hands in mine and waited. I hadn't expected it to end this way, in an antiseptic hospital room. Not that I was naive about my mother's condition, but damn it, this was my mother. She deserved to die in peace, in a place where she was warm and loved.

I sat with her every day, and Carl stayed with her in the evenings. John and the kids popped in and out constantly, offering their special brand of love and support.

To the amazement of everyone, my mother rallied. Who could forget what a fighter she was? As the week progressed, she grew stronger. Slowly, the doctors were beginning to wean her off the tube. By her second week in the hospital, she was breathing—with the help of an unintrusive oxygen-tube nose clip—on her own.

One night the phone rang at two-thirty, and I grabbed the receiver before I had even opened my eyes. My mother's thin voice whispered from the other end, "Gerry, I keep buzzing and nobody comes."

I was fully awake now. "Mom, what's wrong?"

"I need the bedpan, Gerry, and nobody comes."

Where were the nurses? I was alarmed. I hung up the phone and dialed the nurses' desk on my mother's floor. A harried female voice answered after many rings. "This is Geraldine Ferraro," I said sharply. "My mother is a patient on your floor. She just called me at home because she has been ringing for a nurse for a long time, and no one has responded. She needs a bedpan."

"This is a very busy time," the nurse replied. "We're doing the medications. She'll just have to go in the bed."

"What?" I yelled into the phone. "Do you know what that does to a person's dignity? Give my mother a bedpan, and treat her like a human being."

"I'll see what I can do," she replied without contrition, and hung up the phone. I was seething as I pounded my fists against the bed. John, of course, was awake by now, and he tried to calm me down. "We'll talk to them tomorrow," he said. "We'll take care of it." But I couldn't go back to sleep for the rest of the night. The next morning I was at the hospital before eight, and I hired a private nurse to stay with her at night.

My mother was getting thinner and weaker. She didn't seem to be coming back the way she always had in the past. Sometimes she'd lapse into a fit of coughing that was so deep it seemed to tear her insides apart.

One day Dr. Filardi led me into the waiting room and sat down across from me. "It's touch-and-go," he said. "She's a little better than she was when she came in, but I don't see how anything's going to radically change in her favor. The emphysema is just too advanced. You have some decisions to make."

I nodded numbly. "She has a living will. She wants nothing extraordinary done, and I'll go along with her wishes. Nothing extraordinary."

"Okay. No extraordinary measures. Now let me ask you something else. Suppose your mother's heart stops. Do you want her resuscitated? A 'do not resuscitate' order is different from a living will's 'no extraordinary measures.' "

"Let me think about this. I don't know." I really didn't know. I felt a sense of panic. What if I made the wrong decision? I held my mother's life in my hands, and I didn't want to make that decision alone. I had to call my brother.

Carl thought our mother should be resuscitated if her heart stopped. "That's different than putting her on a machine," he said. I agreed. "Okay, let's do that." I hung up the phone and started to walk down the hospital corridor. Something was nagging at me, and by the time I found Dr. Filardi, the thought had taken on a concrete form.

"Doctor," I said, "what happens when you resuscitate someone? I'm ignorant about this. Is it like on television? They put the electric paddles on, and the whole body jumps?"

He said yes.

I felt a sudden surety take hold. "Doctor, look at my mother. Look at her bones. What would happen to my mother if you did that? Would it break her ribs?"

"Between cardiopulmonary resuscitation and electric shock, probably," he said gently.

Oh no, I couldn't accept that—my mother in her last few moments being poked, jostled, prodded, exhorted, lying with her ribs broken like an injured bird. There was no sense to it. That was too much pain. I made the decision. Do not resuscitate.

Several years later, when my daughter Laura was in her last year of medical school and working in the emergency room, a similar case came in—an elderly woman with heart failure. In resuscitating her, the doctors broke several of her ribs. When Laura spelled the doctor in massaging her heart, she could feel them. The woman died the next day. Laura called me and said, "Mom, you made the right decision about Nan."

My mother rallied again. Maybe she was still trying to protect me, with the same instinct that had been so strong all my life. She didn't want me to have to make such a terrible decision. But a better thought occurred to me—it wasn't her time. I was elated as I arranged to bring her home for Christmas. Now I had the opportunity to do what I had been waiting to do all my life—take care of her as she had always taken care of me.

We settled my mother into Donna's old room, on the second floor, next door to the bathroom. We didn't have one on the ground floor. It would have been better for her to be downstairs, but she refused to be carried up and down the stairs to the bathroom.

There is a small terrace right off our bedroom on the second floor, and my mother wanted to sit out there and get some fresh air. It was clear and cold—a typical New York December—and I didn't think it was such a great idea. But she said, "Oh, Gerry, you just bundle me up like I did with you when you were a little baby. We used to sit outside on the coldest days."

I laughed. I thought she was joking.

"Really," she said, twinkling at the memory. "Your first winter. You were four or five months old. My mother always taught me that fresh air is the best thing in the world for you. I'd wrap you up in afghans that I made myself. You were warm as toast, your little cheeks red and healthy."

I shook my head in amazement. You certainly wouldn't find much support among parenting experts these days for sitting outside with a newborn baby in subfreezing weather. But I could well imagine the origins of the practice. When twelve people were living together in three small rooms, the windows tightly shut to capture any heat, the crisp outdoor air might seem like a wonderful tonic.

If my mother wanted to sit out on the terrace on cold December mornings, I wasn't about to deny her the pleasure. I wrapped her in blankets and wheeled her out, and she did seem to breathe easier. I sat with her, reading the newspapers, my nose red, my fingers stinging and stiff. It didn't matter. It was fresh air for my mother.

* * *

Christmas was coming. It had always been my favorite time of year—especially since my mother had gone to great pains to make it that way for me when I was growing up. I decided to make it a simpler celebration than usual because of her health, although I felt tremendously grateful that she would be with us.

When we were getting ready to sit down to dinner, I asked her if she wanted to join us. She said no. When she had first arrived, John had carried her downstairs to join us for dinner, but she refused to let him do it again. Her bones were so brittle that it hurt her to be carried. So I gave her a bell and told her to ring it when she wanted me.

Almost as soon as we were seated, my mother began ringing the bell. And she rang every ten minutes. Each time she rang, I'd pop up from the table and run upstairs. Up and down, up and down. I finally got it. She was lonely. I rushed through dinner and went upstairs to watch some TV with her.

Laura, however, was quite amused by the bell ringing incident. "Gee, Mom," she laughed. "Why didn't we figure this out when we were young? Ring the bell and you come running!"

Several months earlier, I had arranged a special Christmas gift for John—a trip to a baseball fantasy camp in Florida at the end of January. It was sponsored by the New York Mets. I was very proud to have come up with such an imaginative gift, and I couldn't wait to see the look on his face when he found out. John loved baseball with a passion. Every year he and John Jr. played in a softball league at the beach, and when they weren't playing, they rooted for their team, the Mets. It sounded to me like the best feature of the camp was the final day—when they would play a game against former pros, including several players from the 1969 World Series champion Mets.

I already had all the tickets and reservations arranged, of course, but the camp sent a list indicating that I still needed to make some purchases. I swore my son-in-law, Paul, to secrecy, and had him choose the remaining items for me.

On Christmas Day, when we gathered to open our gifts, I placed two packages in front of John. The first contained a beautiful brand-new baseball glove. John thanked me sincerely with his famous—to me—slow smile, but I could tell he was thinking, What's with this woman? Doesn't she know the difference between a baseball glove and a softball glove? The second package contained a pair of cleats. "Oh, these are really great," he quietly enthused. I almost laughed out loud. John had absolutely no use for cleats under ordinary circumstances. Everyone wore sneakers at the beach when they played softball. But I knew my husband. He would never in a million years say he didn't like something that I'd given him.

"These are beautiful cleats, honey. Thank you." John smiled warmly. Finally, as though it had just occurred to me, I said, "Gee, did I forget to give you this? Sorry, John. This is the last one."

I handed him the small package containing the tickets, and he opened it. When he realized what it was, my normally reserved husband leapt out of his chair like an excited kid. We were all laughing, and my mother was beaming. It was a perfect Christmas.

January was cold and gray, but I continued to wheel my mother out to the terrace for her fresh air. Some days she seemed almost back to her old self. Other days she'd look so weak and thin that I thought she'd simply fade away. I dedicated myself to nursing her back to health in the tried-and-true method of Italian women everywhere. I fed her. Day after day, I cooked thick, meaty lamb chops and thin slices of sautéed filet mignon. I tempted her with noodles and pies and her favorite scrambled-egg-and-potato omelet. She barely touched the food, even when I pleaded and cajoled. In denial, I kept cooking, searching for the delicacy that would finally unlock her tastebuds and restore her appetite.

On January 26, the day before he was scheduled to leave for baseball camp, John found me in the kitchen stirring a big pot of soup. He sat down at the kitchen table and said, "Gerry, I'm not going."

I didn't look at him. I just kept stirring the soup. "Don't be ridiculous. Yes, you are."

"No, I'm not. Your mother's not doing well."

I turned from the stove. "She's doing better, John. Look, she's not going to be perfect, but I want you to go. My mother will be all right, and so will I."

I finally convinced him. The truth is, I don't really know what I was thinking. Was I caught up in a child's adamant conviction that my mother would be okay as long as I said she would be? Well, my mother was the woman who always managed to make things happen, who never admitted defeat, and I was her daughter. I wasn't planning on giving in, either, so there were two of us in this battle.

John left the next morning, torn between delighted anticipation of the camp and genuine and affectionate worry for us. I reassured him all the way to the door. It wasn't as if I'd be alone. A nurse came every day and our housekeeper, Ernestine, was there. Carl would come by after work and sit with her. And the kids were always in and out.

With John away, I decided to stay in Donna's room with my mother so I could hear her if she needed me in the night. There was a trundle bed in the room, and I pulled it out and slept only a few feet away from her. Before she went to sleep each night, I had gotten into the habit of sitting with her and holding her hand while she drifted off.

Each day I continued my tempting feeding program—pastina, pancakes, eggs, chops, fish, whatever I could think of. "You gotta eat," I teased her. "If you die and everyone sees you're so thin, they'll arrest me. They'll think I starved you!"

She'd beg me to stop teasing her—it hurt to laugh. And she insisted, "I don't feel good, Gerry. I don't want to eat."

"Just a little bit . . . just eat a little bit," I kept urging her. But I could see that she wasn't just being obstinate. Her body was shutting down. It didn't want nourishment anymore.

That night she whispered across the room, "Gerry."

I came to her side. "What is it, Momma?"

"Come and get into bed with me. Sleep with me." I climbed into bed with her, thinking, If I roll over, I'll squash you, Momma. But my presence seemed to calm her. That night she stayed tucked in close to me, sleeping deeply, her arms around me like a baby.

By Friday morning her breathing had grown increasingly labored, and she'd barely eaten in two days. I sat next to her on the bed and held her hand. "What do you want me to do? Do you want to go to the hospital?"

"I don't know," she whispered.

"Do you want me to call the doctor?"

She nodded.

I got Dr. Filardi on the phone, and he quietly, kindly told me what I already knew. "If you bring her to the hospital we can make her a little more comfortable, but there's nothing much else we can do."

"How would you make her more comfortable?" I asked.

"We'd probably have to intubate her again—put her on the respirator," he sighed. "If we put her back on the respirator, that'll be it. We won't be able to wean her off again. If we do that, it's sort of a final statement."

I reluctantly gave the information to my mother, and for a moment I saw a flash of her old fire. "I'm not going back on that thing," she rasped. "I don't want it. If I need the oxygen, we have oxygen here. I'm not going back to the hospital."

Sister Jean arrived shortly after that, and we sat together with my mother. When the phone rang, I went next door, into my bedroom, to answer it. It was my cousin Jane calling from Florida to see how Mom was doing. I was in the process of telling her when Sister Jean called out to me in an urgent voice. "I gotta go," I told Jane, and hurried back in the room.

My mother was sitting straight up in bed. Her face was lit with a brilliant, joyful smile. Her right hand was stretched out in front of her startled eyes. She was looking away from me and up to the right, reaching out as if she was trying to grab hold of somebody. Sister Jean had her arm around her and was saying the Hail Mary. I ran to my mother's side and held her in my arms as she slipped away. My eyes brimmed with tears. I felt such a surge of faith—of love and hope. Who had she seen at that last second? Had my father come for her? Was it her baby Gerard? I sat holding my mother for a long time, reluctant to let go—of her, of that moment.

John was devastated that he was not there for my mother and me. He couldn't get over it. He kept saying, "I shouldn't have gone. I should have been home." But I finally told him that it had been the way it was meant to be. While he was there I didn't sleep in the room with my mother. While he was there she wasn't able to hold me all night long. While he was there I was his wife, I wasn't her baby. Alone together, we were able to take the time we needed to really say good-bye. John had always been wonderful to my mother, even in this. We had been able to arrange just what she needed for her passing.

• TWELVE •

THE FORGE

Losing my mother was different from losing my father. At eight years of age, I had grieved for the times my father and I would never share. At fifty-four, it was for what would never be again. I had been my father's princess, but my mother had allowed me to be her friend. My mother and I had been together for my whole life. We were so close that it was as if a part of me had been amputated, as if I'd lost an arm or leg.

There was no one who knew me as my mother did. Her particular mix of iron and compassion, her native intelligence, and her striving for something beyond her ability to reach were all brought to fruition in her hopes for me. Her innate goodness and decency were never compromised by the hardships she faced. From the time she'd been a little girl and her own father had been felled by a stroke, she gave far more to her family than she ever received.

Even though my mother had been sick with a variety of ailments for some time, she was still as sharp as a tack mentally. Until the day she died, she'd been cognizant and communicative. Somehow—because I loved her, because I wanted her to live forever—I didn't expect her to go, and when she did, I was heartbroken. There's nothing that can prepare you for the loss, nothing anyone can say to you that makes it any better.

She lived a good life.

She was eighty-five.

At least she won't suffer anymore.

Now she's with your father and your brothers.

None of it helped. For months after she died, I was constantly picking up the phone to call her. All I had to do was think of her and my eyes would fill with tears. I walked around with a knot in my throat for what seemed like years after I lost her. Here I was, a mature woman in my fifties, reduced to a lost child.

The days immediately following my mother's death were filled with frantic activity. I kept myself from falling apart by concentrating on writing a eulogy that would be the tribute she deserved. But on the day of the funeral, I woke up to the realization that I wasn't going to be able to stand in front of the church and deliver the words I'd written. Even though I'd spoken in front of countless audiences, this was different. I knew that I couldn't speak about my mother without breaking down, yet I wanted the words I'd written to be clearly heard and fully expressed. Finally, I called my daughter Donna. I asked her if she would deliver my words for me.

Donna is a strong young woman who has the ability to remain centered and calm when everyone else is falling apart. My firstborn understood the special dynamic that existed between my mother and me, how vital her influence had been in my life. She understood why I found it impossible to do this myself, even though I desperately wanted to. So, she agreed to take my place and read my eulogy.

The funeral Mass for my mother was held at Our Lady Queen of Martyrs Church on February 6, 1990. It was an unusually bright and sunny day, crisp and clear. The comforting prayers of the Requiem Mass stanched the tide of my grief.

> Lift us up, strong Son of God, that we may see further; cleanse our eyes that we may see more clearly; draw us closer that we may know ourselves to be nearer to our loved ones who are with you
>
> Receive, Lord, the soul of your servant Antonetta, and give her the life that knows no age, the good things that do not pass away . . .

When it was time, Donna got up and stood before us. Speaking in a clear voice, she said, "My grandmother had great love for her church. She derived strength and took comfort in its teachings. For each of the priests on this altar she had deep affection. Today, I am sure she is thrilled to see the fuss being made over her. But knowing my nan, I am also positive she is impatiently waiting for her Gerry to get up and speak. And today, probably for the first time in her adult life, her Gerry can't. And so she asked me to express her thoughts to you. This is from my mother."

Donna's eyes locked onto mine for a brief second. In that instant, we had a long, long conversation. About mothers, daughters, love, and duty. About dreams, convictions, and encouragement. About passing on the best of yourself to someone else.

Donna began reading the words I'd written.

"Over the past several years, I have been asked more than once who my role models were. Without hesitation I say, Eleanor Roosevelt and Antonetta Ferraro. Eleanor Roosevelt taught me about life and responsibility on a societal scale. But Antonetta Ferraro taught me about family life and responsibility on a personal scale."

I went on to recount my mother's many contributions. Everything I'd gained had been earned for me by her. I wanted to make it clear that every accomplishment of mine was shared fully with my mother. She was thrilled when I chose to go to law school, thrilled that I kept our family name—first as a lawyer, then as a prosecutor, a congresswoman, and finally a vice presidential candidate. I recounted how her presence when the children were still small had allowed me to return to practicing law in the first place. As a live-in baby-sitter every summer, for three months each year she'd spoiled my kids with homemade pizza, freshly baked bread, and massive doses of her love and good humor.

And in spite of those wonderful memories, I recalled how my heart ached at the unhappiness some of my accomplishments had caused her, the anguish and embarrassment she suffered during the attacks of the 1984 campaign. How did you erase those hurts?

What words could possibly encapsulate my mother's life? What praise would do her justice? The last few sentences of my eulogy were simple.

"My mother was an unusual woman who lived a tough life. No one gave her anything. She earned it. She died the way she lived. In dignity. She leaves behind no debts, no anger, no unspoken words. She leaves an example that quality of life does not depend on material wealth but spiritual. She leaves a host of friends who will remember her. She leaves a family who loved her.

"On Friday, late in the afternoon, my mom went home. She is now with my father and my other two brothers. She was a fine woman, a fine mother, and I will miss her more than I can say."

When Donna had finished reading, she stepped down and sat beside me. With John on one side of me and Donna on the other, I felt them pressing against me, trying to pour their strength into my body. My entire family were towers of support. I stared ahead of me at the dark coffin containing my mother, the flowers a sea of soft colors surrounding her.

The *forge,* I thought. You can make iron malleable in a forge, and shape it anyway you want. My mother always said that Ferraros bend but they never break. Maybe so, but I felt the heat of the forge. My heart was bending that day.

It was a week before I could bring myself to go to my mother's apartment. I dreaded the task of going through her things. When I arrived, it was like opening the door to a still life of what had been her world. Going into each room was like entering a stage set. Everything was just as she'd left it the morning she went to the hospital. The silence and the stillness carried with them an air of finality. And then I opened one of her closets. My mother's familiar scent poured over me. I fingered the fabric of her dresses. Her shoes, a scarf, her gloves. I felt myself beginning to unravel. How could all of this remain and she be gone? My eyes shut against the reality, I leaned in and inhaled deeply, lost in countless memories of the past.

I couldn't go through her clothes just yet, so I shut the closet and began sorting papers instead. I glanced in several files containing insurance and banking information. Then I found a large box, in another closet, that I'd never noticed before. The box was so stuffed with papers that it split open when I moved it and spilled some of its contents on the floor. I sat down on the carpet and began sifting through the pile. What I discovered was fascinating.

Even someone who'd never met my mother would have been able to trace her history, her gains and losses, tragedies and triumphs, by carefully examining the yellowed papers.

The top layer was made up of all of my mother's official documents—marriage certificate, birth certificates, death notices—interspersed with generous helpings of payment stubs and canceled checks, some kept for decades. Why would my mother have kept a 1952 receipt for $50, made out to Shore Hills Estate—a partial payment on a mortgage that had been foreclosed? With a bitter laugh to myself, I remembered anew that I could no longer turn my head and simply ask.

I found her 1905 baptismal record from Saint Lucy's Church on 104th Street discreetly buried under one of Carl's honor roll listings from the New York Military Academy.

A 1940 mortgage for the Mill Street house in Newburgh was on top of the subsequent bill of sale of the same property, from 1946, a couple of years after my father's death. A wage and tax statement from Gold's Bridal Shop for 1970. She made $1,175 that year.

There were cash receipts for chest X rays she'd never told me she had. Mass cards and tiny medals of Saint Anthony of Padua.

But most of all, there was *me*—in infinite variety and at every age: My 1958 ingenue face above a column I wrote in my college paper. A pocket photo album where I'm posed under every plastic page. There were glittery handmade Valentine cards I'd sent to her during my long exile, as well as the program of my Girl Scout investiture, circa 1946, and my first piece of stationery from the House of Representatives. There was a yellowed copy of my wedding invitation, the menu for my reception—featuring prime ribs of beef au jus—and a seven-page itinerary for my honeymoon trip.

Among my writings were efforts only a mother could love. One birthday card read:

> *God has given everyone someone to cherish true.*
> *But never have I met a person quite like you.*
> *So sweet and understanding you always were to me.*
> *And Mom, you've set the pattern of how I want to be.*

In a vinyl autograph book from my junior year, my mother had inscribed:

> To my own sweet daughter,
>
> Since first I held you in my arms, I hoped and prayed you would turn out to be the little lady you are to-day. Darling,

continue on until you have reached the goal I have set before you.

Love, Mom

To keep things from being too sentimental, Carl had added:

Dear Sis:

Remember darling, be good and the Good Lord will always bless you . . . .

If you're not, then I will be forced to bless you . . .
with a brick . . .

Love, Brother

One of my more maudlin poems, written in the voice of a mother who's lost a son in the Korean War, could have been plucked straight from Antonetta's own life. I wrote:

> *As I held him for the last time and touched his curly locks*
> *My eyes filled and I thought of when he played with toys and blocks.*

Going through these papers, I realized that my mother and I had long ago formed our own mutual admiration society, propping each other up, giving each other support and strength. My history was so entwined with my mother's that it was hard to separate us.

My eyes were blurred with tears by the time I finally looked at my watch—I'd been going through the papers for almost three hours. As I began to gather them up, a worn cloth book that I'd never seen before fell out of an old legal envelope. In blue was printed BABY BOOK. On the title page was written: IN BLESSED MEMORY OF GERARD FERRARO, MY BABY'S BRIEF CHILDHOOD.

Inside I found the heartbroken voice of my mother, pouring out the account of my brother Gerard's death in one narrative after the next, as if she had to get it right, to find a way of telling it that might give her peace.

Under *Remarks,* she wrote:

> When Gerard was 3 years old, I had a big party for the dear boy. He was so happy. We had a wonderful time. It started at 12 o'clock and ended at 9 o'clock on account of me having to move to Newburgh next day. Sorry I ever moved. I had hard luck from first day, disappointed about house, disappointed about furniture. Furniture arrived at 11:30 at night, rained all night. Had everything settled in 4 days, then Carl had temperature for two days, then Gerard and Carl had temperature for one week.

Knowing my mother as I had, I could almost hear her voice. She'd never told me about her disappointment with Newburgh, but simply reading her thoughts, I could feel the crush of responsibility, the exhaustion she must have felt caring for her sick boys, the alienation of moving to a new community far from anything familiar.

As I leafed through the Baby Book, the heading *First Day at School* was crossed out, and my mother had continued writing:

> My baby was just one year old, and he was so big and fat that everyone called him Carneria. I was so proud of him, especially that everyone told me he resembled my brother. He was so different than any little boy, so mannerly—a perfect gentle boy. Everyone took notice and loved him because he was so quiet. When he spoke he always left the first letter off his words. He adored me and his dad, and cried terrible the night his dad sailed for Italy.

My lost brother Gerard, the poor dead baby that I had been meant to replace, came briefly alive for me through the grace and fluency of my mother's words. I had never known her to write like this before.

Under *Mother's Record,* she continued in a fresh rush of pain:

> We went out on October 13, 1934, to take baby out for a breath of air. He was just getting well and doctor said be careful for draughts. So I asked doctor if it were okay to take my darling boy out to Highland, and he said yes. So I picked my baby up and kissed him, not knowing it was my last kiss, and dressed him up, not knowing he was never to return home. . . . While coming home that unforgettable Sunday night, we met with an auto accident. . . . I don't recall a thing besides taking my baby from the back. I awoke at home having been unconscious for hours and found a doctor near me, and asked for my beloved baby Gerard, and the doctor told me my baby had died and with him my heart died.

I'd always known the account of my brother's death, but reading her words made the enormity of her loss more real than it had been before. This little book was the place where my mother had been able to register the heartbreak and disappointment that she'd kept from everyone else. I was touched by these pages, seeing how much she had shielded me over these many years. But all of that was over now. She could shield me no longer. As I left her apartment and locked the door behind me late that afternoon, I felt the full weight of her absence.

I was her daughter. I was left to continue her line. Now it was up to me to also continue her dream. For the first time in my life, I would have to do it without her.

• THIRTEEN •

RACING AWAY

It was in the year after my mother died that I began to think about running for the Senate against Al D'Amato. On the face of it, this may have seemed like a crazy idea. Was I really willing to go back into the wringer? In the six years since the 1984 presidential campaign, I had never been able to shake the negatives that haunted me during that campaign.

I knew people felt very strongly about me—they either loved me or hated me. And many of them associated me with my family's problems.

Could I ask John to go through this again?

Again, if John had said no, if he had urged me to stay out of politics, I would have done anything he asked. But my stalwart husband, in his quiet way, believed what I was doing was important.

Had my mother been alive, as painful as my loss in 1984 had been for her, she would have encouraged me. She was a forward-looking woman. She always said that if things didn't work out the first time, move on, and she practiced this courage in her own life. I drew strength from her iron will and determination. And I contemplated the incomprehensible faith of her own mother and my other immigrant predecessors. I could not imagine them turning back from their purpose in life because the path was painful. And neither would I.

You see, the fact that it's a struggle is never a good enough reason not to run. You do it because you believe you can make a difference. You do it because it's an opportunity available to you that could barely have been imagined by your ancestors. You certainly don't do it for money or power—which is the cynical interpretation many people have of politicians and their motivations. You can go broke running for political office, and as for power, well, it's a limited and fleeting thing. An effective representative takes her power from her constituents. The power belongs to the democracy, not to the individual. So the reason you run is that your vocation is public life.

John understood this about me, and he stood by my side. There would be no regrets, no second-guessing later on. In January 1991, I began laying the groundwork for my campaign.

I knew the primary would be tough. Attorney General Bob Abrams had already declared his intention to run, and he was a formidable opponent. He was well known and well liked among Democrats. Even so, I felt that the real question had to be which one of us could defeat Al D'Amato. I thought I was the one for several reasons. First, I was a woman, and D'Amato's status among women voters, even in his own party, was shaky. Second, not only was I a woman, I was an Italian American woman. My support would cut right into his strongest voting bloc. Given the choice, Italian Americans will often vote for one of their own—but what if the choice is between two of their own?

The Italian American community has never been politically unified in this country. You're as likely to see Republicans like D'Amato as you are to see Democrats like me or Mario Cuomo. You can't take the community for granted. They won't fall into your pocket automatically. But that's where my third advantage came in. I knew one thing for certain about Italian American voters—they cared about bread-and-butter issues, about family, about safe neighborhoods, about education. That's what I cared about, too. This would be a campaign about the issues.

I loved being back, although my mother's absence was more deeply felt as I worked the phones and talked to groups across the state. Antonetta had often been my most effective entree—especially at women's groups and senior citizen gatherings. People just fell in love with her. They trusted her. She'd tell them to vote for her daughter, and I swear that's exactly what they did.

I continued to gain ground on Abrams, and even when Liz Holtzman got into the race, my numbers kept rising. As we neared the primary, I was eighteen points ahead and confident of victory.

In retrospect I realize I wasn't fully aware of just how personal this race was for Liz. It was not only important for her to win, it was also important that *I not win.* She felt that there was room for only one woman in New York's political leadership, and that position belonged to her.

In 1980 Liz had lost a heartbreakingly close race against D'Amato that sent him to the Senate for the first time. Now she thought she deserved the chance to make a clear run at him. I think she resented my being in the race, and she was outraged when EMILY's List, a powerful fund-raising organization for women candidates, backed me over her.

By midsummer of 1992, with the primary only a few weeks away, I was holding on to a comfortable lead over Abrams, and Holtzman was running a distant third. Then the *Village Voice* ran a piece about me. To be honest, I didn't think much of it. It was classic *Voice* material—alleging ties to organized crime with an almost laughable attempt to paint me as a supporter of pornography because a tenant from one of John's buildings was using the space to store magazines which *might* include child pornography. The charge was so ludicrous that I didn't even dignify it with a response. Pro-pornography? *Me?* Come on!

But the next thing I knew, there was Liz Holtzman on TV waving the *Voice* article and charging me with "collecting $340,000 from a child pornographer." Abrams joined the chorus, and suddenly the entire election was focused on me and the same old rumblings about the Mafia . . . pornography . . . underground connections. There was no more talk about issues. I had been blindsided.

By primary day Abrams and I were running even. Madeleine Albright came to spend the night with me. For long hours after the polls closed we sat and watched the numbers teeter back and forth between Abrams and me. At ten o'clock Holtzman conceded. "We must work together," she said. "I look forward to working with Bob Abrams." She couldn't resist that last dig, even though the final count wasn't in.

It was two in the morning before Abrams was announced the winner—by a margin of less than 1 percent. I was stunned. I turned to Madeleine. "One percent," I whispered. I was devastated. Madeleine hugged me and offered words of support. We were both political pros. We knew what it was about.

The next morning, Madeleine flew back to Washington and I went to my campaign office. There's no way to describe how cold and empty it feels when you lose. Everyone disappears in a flash. It's over. I sat there and brooded. I had lost before, but this was different. This was wrong. This time I couldn't handle it. Thank God my mother wasn't alive to see this. The bitterness welled up in me. I realized that when you're Italian American you are always vulnerable to being smeared with the innuendos of mob connections. Perhaps we had not come so far after all.

The day after the primary, my campaign manager was contacted by the Abrams campaign. They wanted to know when they could expect my endorsement. They gave me the party rap—it's time for us to come together to defeat D'Amato. But for once I couldn't be the gracious, compliant woman, the good soldier who set aside personal needs for the party. I directed my campaign manager to reply that I would not endorse Abrams until he made a public statement that there was absolutely no basis for any charge that I or my husband were involved with either pornography or organized crime.

I figured I'd get the statement. But the days passed and there wasn't a word.

Donna, who had worked with me on the campaign, finally took matters into her own hands. She told John, "Mom's got to get away. I'm taking her to Florida."

She booked us into the Doral Spa for a week, but even in those gorgeous, mellow surroundings, the angry tape kept playing in my head, and I couldn't stop it. For the first time in my life, I was simply unable to cope. I kept saying, "Why did I do this? I've hurt my husband again and I spent all this money." I could see no silver lining.

At Donna's insistence, I dragged myself to exercise class, but after five minutes I'd be out. I tried getting a massage, but my muscles were knotted into steel ropes. Nothing helped.

Finally, on the fourth day there was a breakthrough. Donna and I were walking by a room where they gave tap dancing lessons. On a whim, she said, "Do you want to tap-dance?"

I laughed. "Donna, I haven't tap-danced since I was a little girl."

She took my arm and began to steer me into the room. "Come on, Mom, you used to force me to go when I was a kid. Let's go together."

In a moment of weakness—or perhaps madness—I relented. We got dressed in our tap costumes—boxy black shorts and T-shirts. I pulled the high-heeled tap shoes over my bulky socks. And we were laughing at the silliness of it.

We walked into the class, and it was full of overachieving, highly competitive women with no wrinkles or sags, and they'd been practicing for days. They had the routines down pat. Donna and I started tapping our hearts out. I was completely focused on what my feet were doing because I knew that if I didn't concentrate I was going to kill myself. For the first time since the primary, my mind was off the race. I was fully consumed by dancing.

We came out of that class laughing, breathing hard, sweating—two girls having a great time. I walked into my room and the phone rang. It was Bill Clinton.

"Gerry," he said warmly, "I want to tell you, I'm sorry about the race."

"Me, too," I said.

"This doesn't mean you should be out of politics," Clinton went on. "I need you. Will you campaign for me?"

My heart lifted. "I'd be happy to."

I was back. I traveled all over the country, stumping for Clinton, talking about the issues, meeting the people, doing what I loved more than anything in the world. It was exactly the therapy I needed.

In New York, Bob Abrams and Al D'Amato were waging a brutal attack campaign. D'Amato is one of the wiliest campaigners you'll ever meet. He took delight in turning the tables on Bob. He started using me in his campaign speeches, talking about how I'd been wronged in the primary. He really turned up the pitch in front of Italian American audiences. It was brilliant the way D'Amato cried out on my behalf, as if he were personally hurt by the way I had been treated.

I wasn't going to stand for that. I wrote a letter to D'Amato and I put it to him straight. Look, I said, I've come through a very difficult time. As far as I'm concerned, Bobby Abrams is terrible. However, as bad as he is, there is no way that I would support you. I consider everything you stand for to be completely reprehensible.

And I told him if I saw him using me one more time, I would go to the press with this letter, and in addition to that, I would endorse Abrams.

I wanted to make absolutely sure D'Amato received the letter personally and that it didn't go to his campaign manager. I knew Al would be marching at the head of the Columbus Day parade, so I got my buddy Ray Kopp, who is a retired detective, to go to the parade with me. The plan was that I would wait in my car and Ray would meet D'Amato as he walked by in the parade.

Now, Ray always wears a gun strapped to his ankle; it's his thing. And as he waited in the middle of the street to give the letter to D'Amato, I saw him start to stamp his foot. What was he doing? I realized that Ray's pants leg had gotten got caught in his gun holster. I nearly died. Old Ray was going to shoot his foot off—I was sure of it. And it would be on my head. Fortunately, he got untangled, ran over to D'Amato, and handed him the letter. Al read it without expression and put it in his pocket. He didn't mention my name for the remainder of the campaign.

Bob Abrams was losing the election. Everyone could see it. I was busy traveling for Clinton, and for the most part I tried to keep my mind off the New York race. But five days before the election, when I was out in California, I received a desperate call from Abrams's campaign manager. I was going to get my letter of apology, and they wanted me to film a commercial for Abrams.

"I can't," I said. "I'm flying into New York Friday evening, and I'll be exhausted, jet-lagged. It's not going to work." But they insisted, so there I was in a studio Friday night with bags under my eyes as deep as potholes. Someone later remarked that I looked as if I had a gun to my head.

The reaction in the Italian American community was instantaneous. My phone started ringing off the hook. "How could you endorse Abrams? Don't you have any pride in your Italian American roots?" They were mad at *me*! It had never occurred to me that my people had felt personally insulted by the unfair allegations against me. Now I saw that the ugly Mafia slur that dogged Italian American candidates was felt as a deep and ever-present wound in the Italian American community. On election day, the Italians flocked to D'Amato. He received 25 percent of the Democratic vote.

Later, when old friends of mine, die-hard Democrats, would whisper in my ear that they had voted for D'Amato, I was shocked by their admissions. Blood really was thicker than politics. I had lost my mother, but I still had my community.

Still, in the back of my mind, my mother's voice was telling me that revenge wasn't the point. Service was. From the grave my mother was continuing my education. I let go of the demons of anger and resentment. This wasn't about me; it was about the people.

After the election, a friend who also happened to be a specialist in bereavement took me aside. "I always advise people not to take on any major changes for two years after a parent has died," she told me. "It probably wasn't a good time for you to run for the Senate."

Maybe she was right. Maybe not. I do know that my mother's death had the effect of energizing me. The collective hopes and prayers, the undaunted drive of this woman and the women who came before her made me more intent than ever to fulfill their dreams. The 1992 election strengthened my resolve. I hear the voices of my ancestors. As long as I have the strength, I can do nothing but fight on in their memory.

· FOURTEEN ·

My Father's House

In 1994, after successful bypass surgery, a pulmonary embolism took my brother, Carl. He was sixty-seven. His last years were physically difficult. His kidneys had been destroyed by years of medication to control his high blood pressure—a problem he inherited from our father—and he was on dialysis. Yet, in many ways his whole life had been difficult. Carl and I had our differences, but it was only after his death that I was able to look at our relationship with some objectivity. I saw that I had been an extremely demanding sister. I wanted Carl to be more considerate of my mother. I wanted him to fulfill his potential. I wanted him to be more successful. I wanted him to be all the things I thought my mother needed to be proud of him. I finally realized that she *was* proud of him. She didn't need him to be different.

In a sense, Carl had spent his life searching for the father he adored, the one who had slipped away from him so suddenly. Being blessed with a son of my own, I'd been able to witness the special bond between a father and son. It has become a lot easier for me to imagine the devastation Carl felt when our father died.

Carl was like our father in so many ways. He resembled him physically, with a strong, burly build and a mop of curly dark hair. He also shared our father's extroverted personality, his effusive style, his warmth. He was a loving and affectionate man who adored his three sons. When Donna gave birth to her first child, Matthew, he was beside himself with joy, as if he too was now a grandfather. The last visit he made to my house, he came in carrying a stuffed rabbit that was twice the size of the baby.

Carl's decision to settle in Italy for so many years seemed to me an effort to understand what had formed our father's life. I always thought it an unusual decision for a first-generation Italian American, especially after having received the finest education and being given every opportunity to succeed in the States. Maybe Carl was torn between the very different cultures of Italy and America. In Italy, the temperament was more Mediterranean, more sanguine, while America was more fast paced and driven.

Carl never seemed to find his place in the world. I think he always felt betwixt and between. At least he would find his final rest with his family in America.

Once again, the family plot at Calvary Cemetery in Queens was opened to make a place for Carl. Now my parents rest side by side, the two tiny coffins of my baby brothers, Anthony and Gerard, above my father. Carl rests above my mother, abutting his twin brother, Anthony's, little coffin.

When I decided to take the job of cohosting CNN's *Crossfire,* my life was once again taking place on the fly, with my shuttling back and forth between Washington and New York. I had never planned to join the media. I'd certainly had my fill of journalists. When a producer at CNN first approached me, I was very skeptical about the idea. First, I wasn't sure if I *could* do it. Second, I wasn't sure if I *wanted* to do it.

And third, I didn't know if it was something I *should* do. The format seemed to encourage arguments; the panelists tried to outshout each other, and I thought that nobody ended up really being heard substantively on any given topic. It was one thing to have a lively and vigorous discussion about the issues, but I thought that the nature of the show seemed too inflammatory and confrontational. I didn't see myself shouting to be heard in a televised slugfest. The producer assured me that they were planning to tone down the confrontations.

Once I accepted the premise of my appearing as a cohost on *Crossfire,* I had a more serious problem. The format involves one host representing the view "from the left" and another representing the view "from the right." But the truth was, I considered myself a pragmatic moderate—my views didn't fit neatly into any single branch of a party line.

"Maybe I'm not the right person for this. You may be disappointed that I'm not a stronger voice for the left," I said. But that didn't matter to him. The point was, I'd have a different voice than the men I'd be facing.

So I took my seat "from the left" on *Crossfire* and was soon sitting across from Pat Buchanan, John Sununu, and occasionally Bob Novak, debating the issues. These were sharp, articulate guys, and I'd always enjoyed a good debate, so it didn't take me long before I was fully engaged in my new work.

The biggest shock for me was that I really liked Pat Buchanan. I suppose that would have surprised anyone who saw how fundamental our disagreements were. But I respected Pat's intelligence, his passion, and his decency. In a sense, he was the brash Irish Catholic kid and I was the fiery Italian Catholic kid, still facing off, each of us trying to gain a larger foothold.

When I wasn't in Washington, I was engaged in an excavation into my past. Tracing the lives of my immigrant forebears was one of the more difficult things I'd ever done, because the search was full of missing links and puzzling details. I knew little at that point about the best way to go about it, so I just started digging. As I pored over records and teased recollections from the few remaining relatives alive, I became fascinated by the work. Why hadn't each family kept records of all of this? But I soon realized the answer. They were eager to get on with it, to flow like blood into the veins of the nation and become a part of it, to find their small space and begin to make a life. Few of them had kept records, journals, diaries—there'd been no time. Many were unable to read or write—what record of their lives could they have left behind?

At the Census Bureau I found my mother's family, the Corrieris. The 1920 census gives the bare details of their lives, printed in a neat hand across a multicolumned form. My grandfather Domenico, sixty years old, had listed himself as a laborer for a steamship company, although by then, disabled by his stroke, he had long stopped working. I assumed that he claimed to be a laborer to save face. As the head of the Corrieri household, it would be embarrassing to say he was retired, or unemployed, and that he therefore made no financial contribution. My grandmother's name appeared in its American form, Josephine. She had replied no to the question of whether she could read or write. The children were listed; I saw my mother's name, a fourteen-year-old Antonetta, already employed as an embroidery operator.

I searched for my father's name at Ellis Island but didn't find it. The records were taken from the steerage passengers, and my father had traveled first or second class.

I visited Mott Street, where the building still stands that was my grandmother's first home in America. I rode the subway uptown, but there is no Italian Harlem anymore. The street that was once bustling with families is now Metropolitan Hospital. The tenements are gone.

As I continued my search, I was slowly able to put the pieces together from both records and memories, until I was able to form the barest frame of my family's lives.

On a visit to Italy in 1996, I had an opportunity to further contemplate my history.

Naples is beautiful in the spring. The old city of 3 million is built on steep slopes raking sharply up from the huge azure blue bay filled with hulking ships. High above, Mount Vesuvius sits to the left, while Sorrento and the isle of Capri are visible over the Gulf of Naples. Naples is such a large port that it's easy to picture the vigorous maritime trade that drove it, the old steamers loading up at the docks and embarking for America, filled with eager, sometimes desperate immigrants.

The port is obviously the centerpiece of the city. Behind enormous, thirty-foot-high gates sit the endless docks at which giant ship after giant ship is tied up. Freighters are moored throughout the vast bay, waiting their turn at the docks. The United States Navy's Seventh Fleet —the Mediterranean Task Force—is also permanently attached here and has its own facilities to maintain its carriers, battleships, cruisers, destroyers, and array of escort ships. The American naval presence in Naples is very minimal and unintrusive—the city itself seems unaffected by it. Almost everywhere you walk in Naples, there is a spectacular view of vibrant blue water set off against the dazzling white cliffs.

I thought about my mother's revelation before she died that she had considered bringing Carl and me back to Italy to live after my father's death. How different my life would have evolved had she done so. I would have been more Italian than American. When my mother first told me about her thought to move to Italy, it struck me as a very odd instinct. My mother, after all, was an American woman, born and bred in the United States. She had visited my father's family in Marcianise early in their marriage, but she had no real connection to the land. Her own family had moved to America.

However, as my mother's letters to my grandparents in Marcianise revealed, she felt bound to them like a daughter. She was the mother of the Ferraro children. By virtue of the children she and Dominick had brought into the world, she was a Ferraro as well. Perhaps she thought that by bringing us to my father's hometown, she could bring their beloved son back to life for his parents. In the back of her mind, there might also have been the hope that by living in my father's land she could in some way restore his memory more fully for herself. And there were no doubt practical considerations as well. She may have felt frightened by the challenge of raising two children alone—worried that she would be unable to provide us with the education and future they had planned. Living in Italy, on property my father had provided, would be easier. She never said a word to me because I was, after all, only a little girl, but I'm sure she missed my father, loved him deeply, and mourned his loss in ways I could never measure. Loneliness and grief might have propelled her across the ocean.

No matter what her initial impulse may have been, she ultimately chose a different path. I imagine she was persuaded by the desire to do the best for us, provide us with the most chances for success—and knew that somehow she would make it happen. Ultimately, she decided that we didn't belong in a small town in Italy. It was more important that she raise us to fulfill the dreams she and my father had. Why return to a nation he had left in pursuit of greater opportunity, a nation in which my American-born mother and her American-born children would have been considered foreigners, inexplicable emigrants from the Land of Liberty—and a place where though her son would have every opportunity, her daughter would not.

I had been to the Ferraro family village of Marcianise on several occasions, and I always made a point of visiting the cemetery where my father's family was buried. I wanted to make a connection with the people I had never known but who were so important to my life.

The cemetery is beautifully manicured, with neatly trimmed hedges lining the maze of alleyways that lead to the various sections.

It is an old-fashioned European cemetery. Instead of flat markers and gravestones, there are small houses—crypts—with ornate gateways leading into chambers where several family members are buried. The name of each family is marked on the front of the tomb.

What always impresses me in this place of the dead is the strong presence of life. Every plot is spotless, carefully tended. Bouquets and wreaths are fresh and have been placed with obvious care. These are people who remain in touch with their dead, who honor them and cherish their memory. There is a small monument in honor of villagers who died during a mistaken American bombing raid in World War II. A fresh bouquet of flowers sits in a small vase beneath the monument. I have been to many American cemeteries, including Calvary in Queens, where my family is buried. Bouquets and wreaths are spotty, more abundant on Mother's Day, Veterans Day, and other special occasions.

At the end of the cemetery, beyond a large white church, is a chapel—La Cappella Congregazione San Pasquale—which belongs to the Franciscans. The chapel is filled with the remains of people of means who had no family crypt. Its walls reach fifteen feet high, lined with the names of those who rest within. Often there are photographs inlaid in the tombs, which is the case with the Ferraros, who are directly inside the front entrance and to the right.

My grandfather Don Carlo is on top, near the high ceiling of the old marble chapel. I can barely make out his features in the photograph. He was much slighter than my father, with small, intense eyes and a thick mustache. He died only a few short years after his Dominick. Below him lies my grandmother Maria Alessandra, who followed her husband to the grave within two years. In her photo she looks stern and imposing. Their children Giuseppe and Amalia are also buried there. Giuseppe was the young Peppino who befriended my mother on her first visit to Marcianise and was killed soon after in an automobile accident.

Amalia's young face stares expressionless from the photograph on her tomb marker. She had died at age twenty-six, and her story was eerily similar to my grandmother Maria Giuseppa's, but with a very different ending.

When Amalia and her brother were still quite young, my grandparents Carlo and Maria Alessandra sent them to America. They were to live with Maria Alessandra's sister, who had no children. Amalia couldn't adjust. She was heartsick at being separated from her family, and she eventually returned home to Italy. Carl, though, decided to stay in America, and his name was changed to Dominic. He ended up becoming a plumber and raising a family in Astoria, Queens. He had two sons, Carl and Nick. It was Nick Ferraro who gave me my start in politics.

My cousins Nick and Carl were both raised to believe that their father had been abandoned by his parents—and to this day Carl will have nothing to do with the Marcianise Ferraros.

If Amalia had only stayed in America, her whole life would have been different. In the mid-1920s, the epidemic *la spagnola,* a deadly Spanish influenza, reached Italy. My grandfather was stricken with the bug and became so ill they thought he would die. His devout daughter Amalia, who was unmarried and had lived with her parents since her return from America, held a vigil for her father, praying night and day for his recovery before a picture of Saint Ann. But nothing seemed to help, and Don Carlo drew closer to death. At one point, when it appeared that the end was near, Amalia turned to her mother. Her eyes were glowing. She announced, "He will survive."

Maria Alessandra was exhausted, overcome with worry and fear. She grew irritated by her daughter's pious posturings. "Foolish child. Don't you see that he is dying?" she snapped. "Be silent!"

But Amalia continued to insist that her father would recover. She remained by his bedside, praying to the picture of Saint Ann.

Miraculously, my grandfather did recover. But just as he rallied, Amalia was suddenly taken ill with the deadly influenza that had almost claimed him. Weakened by her long vigil, Amalia quickly deteriorated. When the priest came to give her last rites, she told him she had been "graced by the Madonna." She died soon after. The picture of Saint Ann to which she had fervently prayed for the recovery of her father disappeared. The family looked everywhere for it, but it was never found. There were whispers of a miracle, suggestions that Amalia had bargained for her father's life by sacrificing her own. The priest who gave Amalia the last rites said she was a saint. Perhaps she was.

My first cousin Maria Tartaglione, my aunt Pasqualina's daughter, still lives in Marcianise. Pasqualina—Lina—was my father's sister. She married Dottore Vicenzo Coliandro, a surgeon and general practitioner. Maria also eventually married a doctor, Angelo Tartaglione. She was always a font of information about the family. Her mother had told her of my father's visits back home to Marcianise. I knew that he had traveled there several times, without my mother, to spend time with his family. My mother refused to make the trip across the ocean with him. After all, on her first visit she had nearly lost Carl, and she wasn't about to take him again. Besides, she had Gerard to care for, and after that, me.

My father's visits were happy occasions for the family. He was much loved and missed, and he always brought gifts for his family and friends. He also bought land while he was there—the land that would later provide money for my schooling—and made sure that all was well with his remaining brothers and sisters. He would always visit the chapel and pray at his siblings' tombs. He was known as a warm, friendly, extroverted man, generous and kind to the people of Marcianise. News of his early death struck the town like a blow.

Maria's daughter Sonja reminds me of my own daughters. She is a beautiful, smart young woman, comfortable in either of our two worlds. Her English is impeccable. Sonja had visited our family in the States and we had become close.

The house in which my father was born and grew up has changed. Where his father had his office is now a butcher shop, *la macelleria.* It is run by the wife of the original butcher—they've been there for forty-eight years now. The living quarters are now inhabited by the butcher's family, as well. The office was empty for a couple of years after my grandfather died, and has been rented out to the butcher ever since.

Across the street from the butcher shop is a delicatessen, a *salumeria.* The building it's housed in was once owned by my grandfather as well.

I discover that my family has expanded beyond Ferraros, to Andrisanis, Tartagliones, and more. Just like so many families before mine, time, emigration, death, and marriage have broadened the family tree to complex and numerous branchings and growths. But breathing the air of my ancestral Italy, talking with the people, seeing the place all make me feel closer to the father I'd hardly known.

Standing high above Naples and looking down over the startlingly beautiful bay only reminds me of what had been forsaken to travel to unknown lands in search of a different life. The gentle wafting breezes off the Mediterranean, the almost tropical land on which I stand, all left behind for weeks at sea to reach America. The unimaginable opportunity that our nation promised drew people as though they were magnetized. Men like my father, who returned home prosperous and happy, with a wife and children, were like shining beacons. "Domenico Ferraro did it. Why can't I?" And he had. He'd come from one level of prosperity in Marcianise to a new level of prosperity in America, and in the process he'd built a whole new life for himself and his family. I inhaled the sweet, warm air of Italy and thought of home—my home in Queens, New York. My home in America. I was looking forward to seeing it again.

When I was young, we were taught in school that America was the great melting pot. The image was vivid—all the nationalities of the world tossed into a bottomless pot and turned into a different dish altogether, blended into a single American people. Complete assimilation was the intent of a largely immigrant culture, because it was clear that those who learned to fit in were the only ones who could make it in America. The attitude became even stronger in first-generation Americans, who didn't have accents like their parents but often were able to talk to them in their native language or use the language as a way to communicate secretly in front of their second-generation children. By the second and third generations, the native language ability became less common, and was usually lost. However, although people assimilated, we each retained our cultural and ethnic identity. The truth was that our nation was never really a melting pot. There was no fire hot enough, no dish that could be cooked long enough to turn us into a homogenous stew. Family trees are characterized by roots as well as branches. I am absolutely an American, and yet my blood is absolutely Italian. I feel no dichotomy, no pull one way or the other. I am from here. I am an American.

There's been a profound change, I think, in the perception of our roots, a reaffirmation of pride in our heritage. We no longer speak of America as a melting pot but as a multicultural nation, rich in diversity. We search for ways to preserve the rich past as we build for the uncertain future. Like a quilt woven from many fabrics and designs, we cherish our ability—unique in the world—to give a common voice to our disparate pasts, to continue to argue our viewpoints with passion buoyed by freedom and a surety grounded in a great history of resolution and change.

We continue to be a nation of immigrants. Furthermore, we are the only nation that welcomes them. It is ironic that Italy, the small country that sent more than 5 million of its citizens to America between 1890 and 1920, now has its own problems with an immigrant population. The relative stability and prosperity of Italy has attracted a swarm of newcomers, most of them from North and

Central Africa, as well as Central Europe. The steady stream of questing humanity searching for a better life has changed the complexion of all of Western Europe. Formerly closed cultures are being forced open, but it is a difficult journey to multiculturalism.

Our own history has shown a fresh wave of conflicts with every new immigrant population. We always managed to resolve our differences and eventually assimilate the latest group—Irish, German, Italian, Russian—into the general population. It has always taken a good deal of time, but it has always happened. When my father came to the United States, there was talk of "the Italian problem," because this new crop of foreigners was so different from those who had come before. Still, the immigrants of my father's era had in common their European roots and their white skin, and America was still young enough to absorb them. Today there is a new uprising of anti-immigrant sentiment, most solidified in states like California, Arizona, and Texas, where residents are fearful of losing what they have built to new arrivals from below the border.

People from around the world still want to come to America. They continue to see our country as the land of opportunity. As we approach the next century, we have yet to make our peace with the impact of continued mass immigration, especially from non-European cultures. Those who cry "America is for Americans" believe that the balance has shifted. Once, immigrants like my father and grandparents contributed to the dynamism and economic prosperity of our nation. They were able to get jobs—working as laborers to create the vast infrastructure of roads, bridges, and tunnels that brought the people of our nation closer to one another; or working in factories to assemble the wonders of the great Industrial Revolution. But the needs of our nation have changed. The industries that drove our nation have changed. Now, it is feared, immigrants will contribute to our nation's demise rather than its continued rise.

I wonder, though, whether the struggle isn't the same one America has always had—a difficulty welcoming nonwhite, non-Western immigrants into its community. Today, of the 24.6 million Americans who are foreign born, fully 25 percent are Mexican. The majority of immigrants come from the Philippines, Cuba, Mexico, El Salvador, and the Dominican Republic. They come from China, Vietnam, India, and Korea. Many are well educated and were professionals in their countries. Others are poor, have little education and few skills.

Illegal immigrants provide a tremendous pool of "cheap" labor that drives an enormous underground economy. The food industry, the garment industry, construction, landscaping, migrant workers—all labor-intensive jobs—are filled with illegal immigrants. It is a problem we have not yet found a way to solve. All people living in our nation need protections, guarantees, a safety net to keep them from falling through the cracks. But our hearts seem to have hardened throughout the nation. Strict initiatives designed to combat illegal immigration also seem to punish legal immigrants for choosing to come here.

To deny people opportunity is antithetical to the very premise of America, the clear promise of America. We are a nation built on the backs of millions and millions of immigrants—how can we now turn around and put up our hands? How can we say, "Stop! Basta! Enough!" What do we really want? Inclusion or exclusion?

Sixty-six years passed from the day my grandmother Maria Giuseppa Caputo stepped onto American soil to the day I, her granddaughter, graduated from college, a completely American young woman. Within a century of her arrival, her two great-granddaughters would achieve academic success at schools she had never heard of, much less dreamed of attending—Donna earning an MBA from Harvard and Laura an MD from the University of Chicago. One hundred years. It is not an unusual immigrant success story of the twentieth century—shared by Irish, German, and Scandinavian families across the nation. But what can a woman arriving in America today expect for herself, and for her daughter? What can she expect for her granddaughter? How long will it take her family to thrive here? What is it that will move a family from a tenement with a toilet in the hall to a country home in Litchfield, Connecticut?

The key is something my mother, in her innate wisdom, understood better than anyone else I've ever known. And she passed it on to me.

"Educate a boy, you educate a boy alone. Educate a girl, you educate a family."

It was clear that education was a priority in our lives from the moment we began our schooling. My parents would have it no other way. Carl was sent to New York Military Academy because of its rigorous academic standards and its intense discipline, and I was sent to convent schools because my parents instinctively knew that my best chance at a superior education lay in the hands of the nuns. My father had arrived from Italy with a distinct advantage; his family prized education, and it was natural for him to desire the same for his own children. My mother didn't even think of abandoning their plans for us when he died. If anything, it made her all the more resolute to see our education continue to the highest levels possible.

My own life had been immeasurably enriched by the education I'd received, and it was a renewed priority for me as a mother with children. I saw to it that each of my children received the very best education. By extension, this became a passion for me in my political life. It was clear what disaster followed in the lives of those deprived of a quality education, what an unfillable void the lack of schooling created, sometimes forever.

In her insightful book, *Within Our Reach,* Elizabeth Shorr offers sobering evidence of the consequences of a lack of education. According to Shorr, the majority of teenage parents, homeless, welfare recipients, the unemployed, drug abusers, and those involved in criminal activity share one common trait: They dropped out of school. It seems to me that if we can convince children that school is the key to their success, not only will we be doing what's right for them but we will also be addressing the most pressing problems in our society. Education will make our nation stronger.

That's true, both for the children born here and for those arriving each day—not at Ellis Island after a monthlong boat trip in steerage, but at airports from coast to coast by jet. Immigrant children, too, deserve a fair chance to grow intellectually and to compete.

We are still a nation of immigrants. Our schools bear the hopes and dreams of immigrant parents. This reality was made strikingly personal to me in the spring of 1998, when I was running for the Senate. I was invited to two schools to see some of the ways that federal dollars were being spent. Intermediate School 125 in Queens has 1,730 students from between sixty and seventy-five different countries. They speak forty-seven different languages. I was there to attend the play, *Richard III,* performed by sixth graders and produced by the cast of Theater for a New Audience—a group of professionals who perform Shakespeare and volunteer their free time to work with the children of New York. Loving Shakespeare, I was delighted to be there. I was also impressed that for a majority of kids performing, English was a second language. As I listened to the familiar words, I thought back to my mother and her friends memorizing Portia's speech from *The Merchant of Venice.* And it dawned on me that Shakespeare has long served as a third language in our schools. It levels the playing field for immigrant children who struggle with English, because their American-born classmates also struggle with the Shakespearean dialogue. I suspect that is why they taught it at P.S. 150 in 1919, and that's why it makes sense to teach it today.

Shortly after visiting I.S. 125, I was invited to be "Principal for a Day" at Public School 160 in Brooklyn.

P.S. 160 is similar to a lot of other public schools in urban areas. There are children from thirty different countries, who speak seventy languages and dialects.

Eighty-five percent of the children qualify for the federal lunch program, and 15 percent of them get to school early each day for breakfast. If they arrive late for school, they have nothing to eat. A lot of the students wear uniforms, although it's not mandatory. A fourth-grader told me shyly, "I like it. It's nice, it's clean, and it makes me feel good." I thought back to my uniform days at Mount Saint Mary's and smiled.

There aren't enough classrooms. A custodian's closet is a reading room for eight kids. It's windowless; they keep the door open for air during class. The old gymnasium, which wasn't that big anyway, is divided by makeshift walls and is used for two classrooms. There are three prefab trailers parked each day in front of the school that serve as mobile classrooms. The science teacher stores her supplies in the corners of the various rooms she teaches in. She has no permanent science lab, and no equipment.

The classes range in size from twenty-eight to thirty-five children. There are five kindergarten classes, but there are enough children to fill six. The prekindergarten Head Start group is filled to capacity, with a waiting list of qualified children. There is only one English-as-a-second-language class, being taught by a Chinese American teacher. The children in the class will be mainstreamed as quickly as possible—first, because there's a shortage of ESL teachers, and more important, because the children are excellent students and are ready to enter the general school population.

My day as principal was exhilarating. There was a wonderful atmosphere in the classrooms and in the halls of P.S. 160, a sense that the teachers and the students were engaged together in a positive educational process, in spite of their many shared difficulties.

During lunch, I met with the teachers during two different periods. "If I had a magic wand," I said, "and could grant you one wish, what would it be?"

"More classrooms!" said the first group.

"Smaller classes," said the second.

No one said "More pay for teachers". . . "respect". . . "more teaching assistants." They cared only about the children. Their hearts were in their work.

I believe that it is the job of government to serve these needs—not as a magic wand, but as a partner in building a common future. Our prosperity as a nation is hinging on our ability to bring all of our citizens into the light of possibility. We can begin right now with some practical efforts: More teachers can be provided by offering partial forgiveness of student loans to college graduates who choose to become teachers. We must repair the deteriorating infrastructure and fully fund the Head Start and school lunch programs. Nationwide, the English-as-a-second-language programs have got to be revitalized. Inclusion is the only glue that will hold us together.

My day as principal of P.S. 160 ended with an assembly program of fourth- and fifth-graders from twenty different countries. I could have closed my eyes and seen little Antonetta Corrieri standing with her classmates, absorbing the history of this country so that she could go home and report to her mother in Italian what she had learned—and perhaps too shy to tell others why her parents had come here. But the children at P.S. 160 told me. They came to America for a chance at a good home, a good job, and a good education. They didn't come for a hand*out*—they came for a hand *up*.

Each of the children gave a greeting in his or her native language, translated the greeting into English, and then performed a traditional dance from his or her country. I joined the children representing Puerto Rico, the Dominican Republic, and Cuba in the merengue. However, when the Russian children started dancing the kazatsky, I got out of the way! The assembly ended with all of the children waving the American flag, the Stars and Stripes, and singing "Come to America." It was so sweet, their faith in this country so deep, my eyes filled with tears.

Surely the most patriotic thing we can do is to educate these children—to offer them a piece of our abundance as it was once offered to our own ancestors. This would be a fitting legacy for all the hopes and dreams our parents and grandparents and great-grandparents poured into factories, sweated out in fields, and hammered out building highways and bridges. They toiled for one purpose—that their children could inherit a better life. My admiration for my grandmother, my love for my mother, only deepened as I looked back on their lives. Could I have been as selfless? Could I have been as strong?

In 1990, shortly after my mother died, I set up a scholarship fund at Marymount College in her name. When I was asked about the criteria for recipients, I replied, "Only that they come from single-parent homes and their mothers need the help."

In eight years, eleven young women have benefitted from my mother's dream.

"Educate a girl, you educate a family." Antonetta would be proud.

INDEX